mothers of invention

Also by Ewan Whyte

Desire Lines: Essays on Art, Poetry and Culture
Shifting Paradigms: Essays On Art and Culture
Catullus: Lyric, Rude, and Erotic
Entrainment: Poems

mothers
of
invention

Essays on the Community of Jesus
and Grenville Christian College

Ewan Whyte

WOLSAK
& WYNN

© Ewan Whyte, 2025

No part of this publication may be reproduced, stored in a retrieval system or transmitted, in any form or by any means, without the prior written consent of the publisher or a license from the Canadian Copyright Licensing Agency (Access Copyright). For an Access Copyright license, visit www.accesscopyright.ca or call toll free to 1-800-893-5777.

Without limiting the author's and publisher's exclusive rights, any unauthorized use of this publication to train artificial intelligence (AI) technologies or systems is expressly prohibited.

Published by Wolsak and Wynn Publishers
280 James Street North
Hamilton, ON L8R2L3
www.wolsakandwynn.ca

Editor: Noelle Allen | Copy editor: Jen Hale
Cover and interior design: Jennifer Rawlinson
Cover image: Xander_D/iStock Photo
Author photograph: Gary William Ogle
Typeset in Adobe Caslon Pro, Antina and Corbel
Printed by Rapido Books, Montreal, Canada

The publisher gratefully acknowledges the support of the Canada Council for the Arts and the Ontario Arts Council. We also acknowledge the financial support of the Government of Canada through the Canada Book Fund and the Government of Ontario through the Ontario Book Publishing Tax Credit and Ontario Creates.

Every effort has been made to contact and request permission for images reproduced and material quoted within this text. All reproductions are made with the utmost respect. We apologize for any errors or omissions that may have occurred. Please get in touch with Wolsak and Wynn Publishers, Ltd., if you wish to discuss any of the images appearing within this text.

Library and Archives Canada Cataloguing in Publication data is available upon request.

ISBN: 978-1-998408-23-8

This book is for the children of the Community of Jesus and the former students of Grenvill Christian College.

And for Peter Andersen, who has always tried to help them.

Isolation is that impasse into which men are driven when the political sphere of their lives, where they act together in the pursuit of a common concern, is destroyed. . . .

While isolation concerns only the political realm of life, loneliness concerns human life as a whole. . . . Totalitarian domination as a form of government is new in that it is not content with this isolation and destroys private life as well. It bases itself on loneliness, on the experience of not belonging to the world at all, which is among the most radical and desperate experiences.

– Hannah Arendt, *The Origins of Totalitarianism*

Contents

Author's Note 1
Introduction 3
The Cult that Raised Me. 7
The Origins of the Community of Jesus 25
The Founding of Grenville Christian College 53
The Art of Deception: The Arts, Music and Poetry of the
    Community of Jesus and Grenville Christian College. . . . 65
Notes on Attending the Civil Trial Against Grenville
    Christian College 85
A Discussion Between Ewan Whyte and Suzan Ewton
    About Her Experience at the Community of Jesus 99
Aaron Bushnell, Trauma and How the Body Keeps
    the Score 117
Episodes in Cult Chasing 127
Landscapes from the Back of a Train: A Personal Essay
    of the Memory of a Cult Childhood. 151

Acknowledgements 165
Notes. 167

Author's Note

These essays, written over fifteen years in different styles, contain descriptions of painful (and/or possibly triggering) subject/topics such as manipulation and abuse – including child abuse and sexual abuse – either as I experienced them or as these stories were shared with me as I conducted extensive research on the Community of Jesus and Grenville Christian College.

Over many years I have compiled hundreds of hours of recorded "on the record" interviews with many people who have been (and some still are) members of the Community of Jesus and many former students and staff at Grenville Christian College. (This is to preserve many people's stories, even if they are not made fully public – like Heidi Laser's dramatic escape from the Community's Bermuda estate with the U.S. Consul in Bermuda, recounted by her cousin in his own voice, and how he brought the Consul with him, as well as other recorded accounts of the same story.) My archive, collected along with Professor Ruth Marshall of the University of Toronto, includes extensive documents, vintage videos and many photographs going back to the 1950s. It grows every year. I have taken every precaution to hide the identities of anyone who did not want to be named (who is not already publicly named or a public figure) in this book. I also avoid naming some current members as they are low ranking and that would not fare them well in their already difficult lives.

Introduction

On November 16, 2023, the sixteen-year class-action lawsuit against Grenville Christian College finally came to a close. As a former student, I could hardly believe it. The infamous boarding school, which was located just outside Brockville, Ontario, and its close affiliate, the Massachusetts-based Community of Jesus, had seemed too powerful to defeat. Its leaders had used incredible deceit and their pull with powerful and wealthy donors to silence students for decades. In the U.S., high-profile members of the Community of Jesus included evangelical notables David Manuel, author of a controversial Christian version of American history; Peter Marshall Jr., the evangelical speaker and Manuel's co-author; William Kanaga, who was Chairman of the Advisory Board of the New York firm Arthur Young and was later Chairman of the U.S. Chamber of Commerce; and at least one member of the Rockefeller family.

In Canada, the film producer Sir Arthur Chetwynd was a supporter, as was Trevor Eyton, the Ontario businessman and senator. Three successive lieutenant-governors of Ontario – Pauline McGibbon, John Black Aird and Lincoln Alexander – all sat on the school's board. Another former lieutenant-governor, Hal Jackman, even gave a commencement speech at Grenville. These dignitaries would likely have been shocked if they had known what happened to the school's students.

Many of the school's former students – some of whom were the children of the province's elite – reported varying levels of maltreatment at the hands of the school's administration and staff, including severe corporal punishment, constant verbal and emotional abuse, sexual harassment and sexual abuse, yelling, scapegoating, shunning, sleep deprivation, forced manual labour and isolation. As a student there I was assaulted, isolated, thrown down a flight of stairs, repeatedly kicked, deprived of food and sleep, locked in walk-in freezers, forced to sleep in soiled bedding for a week, sexually harassed and witnessed sexual assault on children. It comes as no surprise that the effects of the abuse followed many students into adulthood.

The extremely high suicide rate of former students is deeply distressing.

I spent three long years at Grenville in the 1980s, during Grades 7, 8 and 9. Before that, I was a forced child member of the Community of Jesus. Both of my parents were members of this "church," which was founded in Massachusetts in 1970. It is by far the most extreme of the three original surviving Covenant communities from the Charismatic Renewal in the United States, which started in the early 1960s and picked up steam as a backward-looking reaction to the late 1960s Flower Power movement. The founders of the Community, Cay Andersen and Judy Sorensen, used punitive mind-control techniques, called "light-sessions," on their followers, a mechanism that became the glue that held the leadership together and forged bonds of loyalty among members. The effects on children were devastating.

Cay and Judy, armed with this technique and meeting the fringe group of vulnerable adults at the school that would become Grenville, convinced the staff to become members of the Community of Jesus and live by its extreme lifestyle. This included eventually taking vows of obedience to them for life. In effect, this was, and still is, what I would describe as a micro-totalitarian society. Many inside cannot see it and many former students years later don't fully understand what happened to them.

The school closed in 2007, and its sins were exposed in the mainstream media shortly thereafter. Some former students soon launched a civil class-action lawsuit against the school and the estates of two of its late headmasters. The lawsuit only finally went to trial in 2019.

I was not the only former student who came to watch the trial unfold. Others came from across Canada and the U.S., filling the seats of the courtroom. Some came to hear former students finally detail the horrors of what they had lived through but had never been able to say out loud. They – we – wanted the outside world to know what we had experienced all those years ago, so it would not happen again. I remember that when a clinical psychologist and expert witness acknowledged the significance of the impact of abuse on the lives of so many of Grenville's former students in her testimony, many of the former students in the packed courtroom burst into tears. Several had to leave the courtroom, overcome with emotion. It was a moment when, for the first time, someone in a position of authority had acknowledged what we went through.

Justice Janet Leiper issued her decision on February 23, 2020, and in a reiteration of everything we'd gone through, everything the former students had alleged, she found in favour of the plaintiffs. The judge's decision was appealed by the defendants, but upheld in 2021.

The seventy-five-page ruling also explained the school's financial and spiritual involvement with the Community of Jesus. Donald Farnsworth, the son of long-standing Grenville headmaster Charles Farnsworth, testified that the school gave about $100,000 every year to the Community, and had even purchased a house inside its compound. Ms. Andersen and Ms. Sorensen sat on the board of the school.

The Superior Court of Justice of Ontario ordered that $10,875,000 be paid in damages. The money for each student after sixteen years of legal battles was negligible since the school had been run illegally for many years without insurance. After costs were subtracted, the total was $6,628,781 divided between roughly 1,360 students. But we hadn't pursued justice for the money. We had wanted to be heard.

The prospects for many school alumni are grim, with an

alarming incidence of suicide, addiction and lifelong mental-health issues, all hallmarks of severe trauma. Still, the closure we were offered on November 16 was a victory.

"This settlement is a huge relief and verifies and validates everything I had been trying to tell my family and friends for decades about how the school treated us without our parents' knowledge or consent," Liz Goldwyn, who was a student in the 1980s, told me afterward.

Despite the trial, and hours of testimony from former students and staff, many enablers I have confronted have been dismissive, in complete denial or have refused to acknowledge anything happened at Grenville. I believe the highly addictive nature of the light-sessions has convinced many people that they had participated in something truly spiritual. I do not agree – nor do many of the plaintiffs who won the suit against Grenville.

While it has lost some of its influence, the Community of Jesus remains in operation, obfuscating its links to Grenville and the successful class-action suit. To the children still trapped inside the Community, as I once was: We have not forgotten you.

The Cult that Raised Me

When I was eleven, my parents sent me to Grenville Christian College, a prestigious Anglican boarding school in Brockville. It turned out to be a perverse fundamentalist cult that brainwashed, abused and terrorized students. For decades, the school tried to intimidate us into silence. It didn't work.

Grenville Christian College was an Anglican boarding school a few hundred metres from the St. Lawrence River, just east of Brockville. At its centre was an impressive four-storey stone building, originally built as a junior Catholic seminary in 1918. There was a large chapel on the west end of the building and some new additions on the east, with several trailer homes behind the school, hidden from view. It was summer in the 1980s, and I had just been moved to Ontario from the Community of Jesus in Massachusetts and was now briefly staying with my parents in rural Ontario, in a

Postcard of Grenville Christian College.

small town near the Quebec border. My mother told me we were just visiting – that we were going to see the headmaster, Charles Farnsworth, who would provide me with what she called "child guidance and correction."

We met with Farnsworth in the school cafeteria. He was a short, angry, small man, with greasy black hair and a pronounced Georgia drawl. He wasn't particularly articulate; I remember, even at my young age, being surprised that this person could be a headmaster at such an impressive school. My mother told Farnsworth I needed correction because I'd asked for a pair of jeans and to wear my hair longer than a crewcut. All I wanted was to fit in with other kids. When I requested these things, my mother said they were "the way of the world," which was sinful.

Farnsworth responded by proudly telling us about his experience beating children. He spoke of it with a sense of delight, explaining how he whipped his own sons with a belt, and how good it was for them. He boasted about how he would frequently paddle students at the school. He sounded like a sports fan describing a game, going over the plays, the outs, the runs. About children, he said, "You have to break their spirit." He was terrifying.

When we drove away from Grenville that day, I never expected I would return. My parents were too poor for me to attend the school, so I figured I was safe. A number of months after our visit, my mother excitedly announced that I was going to be a boarding student at Grenville, and that she would be teaching English and remedial reading there. What I didn't understand at the time was that this expensive, impressive school, marketed as a respectable Anglican institution where wealthy Torontonians could send their children, was nothing of the sort. It was a cult.

I would spend the next few years enduring violence, isolation, humiliation and brainwashing at Grenville. It would take almost twenty-five years before this culture of abuse became public – and another decade before I and some 1,359 other former students got something resembling justice.

I was not a happy child. When my parents weren't belittling me, they ignored me. My father was an ordained pastor with the United Church of Christ USA, while my mother was a devout Christian from North Carolina who'd taken courses in literature at Harvard and earned an MA in education from Boston University. Often moody and detached, she seemed to resent being a mother. She was also caught up in the Charismatic Renewal, an interdenominational movement that borrowed many elements of Pentecostalism and promised a personal, emotional connection with God that would inspire a Christian lifestyle.

The Community of Jesus, a Christian commune on the shores of Rock Harbor in Cape Cod, attracted some of the biggest players in the Charismatic Movement. When I was eight, my mother convinced my father to join the Community, which she'd heard about through one of her acquaintances. It was founded by Cay Andersen and Judy Sorensen, two American housewives who'd visited the Evangelical Sisterhood of Mary, a Christian commune in Darmstadt, Germany, and decided they wanted to start an American version. At the Community of Jesus, Andersen and Sorensen anointed themselves as "Mothers" and copied every aspect of the Evangelical Sisterhood, from their strict ideas of discipline right down to the fonts on their brochures. My mother moved us there for a year and a half, and I was forced to live in a house of unhappy boys, only rarely seeing my parents. The Mothers called parental love "idolatry" – the sin of loving anybody or anything aside from God – because they believed it made parents blind to their children's transgressions.

Andersen and Sorensen claimed to "see things in the Spirit" about people or a situation, and said that God spoke directly to them about our sins and atonement. Everyone was subjected to frequent, sometimes daily "light-sessions," in which adult members sometimes spent hours publicly berating and humiliating the victim until they broke down completely. They were called light-sessions because they were supposed to help us "live in the light." At the Community, I found only brief moments of peace – looking out at the salt flats, walking through shrubs lining the paths toward the water and, most of all, in lines of poetry. Poetry has always been an escape, a friend. I started secretly memorizing at least one poem a week when I was quite young. They became part of me, part of how I related to words, meaning and time. These brief moments of eternity were short respites from the fear and pain that were woven into all aspects of my daily life. When I was ten or eleven, my father – by then not an enthusiastic acolyte of the Mothers – convinced my mother to leave. By this point, the child I was when I'd first arrived at the Community had been erased. The loneliness was crushing.

Just as my mother promised, I began my Grade 7 year at Grenville Christian College in the fall. Almost immediately, I knew that most of the staff and teachers there were Community of Jesus people. I had seen many of them at the commune in Cape Cod, including Charles Farnsworth. I'd seen their rings – flat gold, with a Jerusalem-style cross stamped out of it. I knew they had sworn vows of obedience to the Mothers. I soon learned that my mother had struck a deal with Andersen and Sorensen: she'd become a teacher at Grenville, I'd attend as a student and my father would find a parish nearby. At Grenville, children were subjected to extreme verbal, physical, psychological and sexualized abuse, all in the name of the Community. We were beaten with paddles, publicly humiliated, creatively punished for a range of incomprehensible "sins." We were isolated from our families and from each other.

The school's headmaster, Charles Farnsworth, was an acolyte of the Community of Jesus, the Christian commune in Cape Cod. Running the show alongside Farnsworth was his co-headmaster, Al Haig, who'd become involved with the Charismatic Renewal. He'd been a teacher at Albert College in Belleville before his enthusiasm for speaking in tongues and talking about the movement of the Holy Spirit got him fired. He moved to New York to work for Norman Vincent Peale – Donald Trump's one-time pastor and the author of the controversial book *The Power of Positive Thinking*. Haig later ran a Pentecostal school out of a basement in Brooklyn.

Haig met Andersen and Sorensen in the 1960s, and was impressed by the Mothers' preaching: The women once prayed for the Haig's family dog, supposedly curing it from distemper. A few years later, Haig and Farnsworth were working at the struggling Berean Christian missionary school that would later become Grenville. When the Mothers visited the school in 1973, Haig took their trip as a sign of divine intervention. From then on, the staff dedicated themselves to following the Mothers' teachings. The majority of the staff (I remember it as all staff members without exception) took vows of membership to the Community of Jesus, attended retreats at their compound on Cape Cod, wrote reports to the Mothers and tithed 10 percent of their earnings to the Community.

It was around this time that the Anglican bishop in Kingston ordained both Haig and Farnsworth as ministers. On average, according to their account, the school paid $100,000 each year to the Community, and the Mothers appear as directors on Grenville's Ontario letters patent. In around 1983, Farnsworth took sole leadership. His henchmen were known as the A-Team, and his son, Donald, later taught math at the school and served as dean of men.

Like the Community, Grenville was organized around a rigid hierarchical structure. Orders from the top were akin to the word of God, and punishment was administered based on Farnsworth's whims. Students with influential parents received more care, while staff children like me were disciplined with impunity.

Light-sessions were the main form of punishment and control at Grenville. They were used when students committed serious violations, like smoking or stealing, but also to humiliate bedwetters or students caught masturbating. Even trivial infractions – being alone with a student of the opposite sex or simply having a bad attitude – were punished in this way. Staff would haul the offending child up in front of the whole student body and berate them for their "sins," which were often incomprehensible to us – things like haughtiness, rebellion, hiddenness, covetousness, lustfulness. Sometimes these sessions would take place in the chapel or dining room, where everyone could see everything, and students might even be encouraged to participate in the shaming. Other times, the punishment was in private with one or several adults, who would put their faces an inch away from the child's and scream at them as loudly as possible – condemning, shaming, terrorizing. Farnsworth would occasionally take students to the boiler room and push them close to the open flames as a glimpse of the hell they were destined for if they continued to sin. Always there was the threat of physical violence, and then there was violence.

Light-sessions often involved physical abuse too. At Grenville, they used a long wooden paddle resembling a cricket bat. Staff kids and low-status boarders were beaten so hard that they bled, urinated on themselves or could no longer stand. This was what was going to bring children into the light and make us true disciples.

I was subjected to countless light-sessions over my years at the Community and Grenville. Once, at the Community of Jesus, I was feeling unwell at dinner and told the adult members in charge – whom we were forced to call Aunt and Uncle – that I thought I might throw up. I was told to eat what was on my plate: "We will beat you if you don't." I suddenly vomited on my plate and then on the floor. One of the adults struck me on my back repeatedly and screamed at me to eat it. By the end of the ordeal, I was scooping it off the floor and into my mouth with my hands. Another time, at Grenville, I was locked in the walk-in freezer for over an hour as punishment.

I knew I could not be friends with any of my fellow students. The staff created networks of informants: They extorted us to tell on each other for any transgression, supposedly to help our friends "see the light." There was a lot of incentive to rat each other out – when we did, we were showered with praise and, best of all, kept out of the hot seat, at least for that day. There was little trust among the staff children, who were alternately pitied and shunned by the paying students. Even if close friendships did emerge, they were quickly broken, as friendship was considered a form of idolatry. Meanwhile, I rarely saw my mother. She lived in staff quarters, while my father lived in his parish nearby. I, on the other hand, slept in a cramped mobile trailer around the back with other staff children. When I did see her, I knew better than to complain. Her allegiance was to Grenville and the Community of Jesus, not to me. I was completely alone.

Another central feature of Grenville life was the punishing schedule of daily activities. First there were morning assemblies, which sometimes devolved into spontaneous light-sessions involving the entire school. Then chapel, classes, extracurricular

Children washing the dock at Grenville, 1990s. Photo credit and permissions: Mel Childs.

activities, late-night study hall and the dreaded unpaid "work-jobs." We worked in the kitchen, served meals, cleaned the dorms, kept up the grounds, built and maintained structures – mostly during our so-called free time – after school and on weekends. Sometimes we were assigned jobs as a form of discipline, or "being on D." Staff removed the child from class, forbade them from speaking to other students and forced them to complete the most difficult, menial or demeaning jobs until they were deemed sufficiently repentant.

Students were often made to help with the upkeep at Grenville, like cleaning the dock, as pictured above.

Being on D could last from a day to a month for paying students, while staff children were sometimes put on D for entire semesters. We'd scrub pots in the kitchen, pound stakes, shift rocks, clear ice, clean bathrooms with a toothbrush. I remember cutting a section of the lawn with scissors. It was hopeless and absurd, but I had to cut away until a staff member or a prefect decided I'd had enough. It's stunning just how much of the regular upkeep of Grenville was done by students – it certainly must have saved them a lot of money. There was almost no free time for us to simply relax and be children. This labour stunted the imagination and compounded our loneliness. We lived in a constant state of stress, exhaustion and fear, all of which helped ensure emotional and spiritual compliance.

The most incredible part of the Grenville story is the fact that its systemic child abuse went on, unknown to authorities, for more than thirty years. To prospective parents, Grenville billed itself as a respectable Anglican boarding school with a strong relationship to the Anglican Church. Henry Hill, the Anglican bishop of Ontario, was an episcopal visitor at the Community of Jesus. A later bishop, Peter Mason, also knew about the Community connection.

David Ardill, a paying student who attended Grenville in 1979, told me that his mother had no idea what the school really was when she sent him there. "Its true nature was all disguised. I would never have been sent there if my mother knew it was a crazy cult school. She was a straitlaced Anglican. They flew the Anglican flag. They read from the Anglican book. Wore the Anglican garb," he said. The Anglican Church, however, denies any authority over Grenville Christian College. When approached for comment, they referred to a 2012 judgment that found that the diocese never had any jurisdiction or power over the school's operations, administration, affairs, staffing, funding, enrolment, discipline or other student affairs, education criteria or curriculum. "The diocese assigned no tasks, had no power or control or legal right to intervene in the operation of the school," they said.

Former prime minister Brian Mulroney with headmaster Charles Farnsworth, 1985 Grenville yearbook.

In the 1980s, when I attended Grenville, I'd heard that tuition was around $20,000 per year. Many illustrious and wealthy Toronto families sent their children to Grenville, and the board was a who's who of old-money Ontarians, the kind of people whose lineage goes back to the Family Compact. They attended lavish dinners and gave commencement speeches and made generous donations. Sir Arthur Chetwynd, a Toronto-based aristocrat with ties to the Empire Club of Canada and the Royal Commonwealth Society of Canada, was a powerful promoter, introducing many friends to the school and sending his grandson there for a year. The Royal Commonwealth Society funded an obstacle course at Grenville in Sir Arthur's name in 1990, and the 1993 Grenville yearbook was dedicated to him and his wife.

Trevor Eyton, the Ontario senator who worked at Torys and sat on the boards of Coca-Cola, GM and Nestlé, was a strong supporter of the school. The singer Tommy Hunter sent one of his sons there. Rosemary Sexton, the Toronto socialite and *Globe and Mail* gossip columnist, was also a cheerleader for Grenville. She sent two of her kids to the school, and I remember her daughter receiving the special care given only to children of the rich and powerful. "The school itself had some wonderful programs and dedicated staff, and many students derived much benefit from attending," she told *Toronto Life*. "That is not to diminish the suffering that those who were abused went through, which was egregious and unwarranted."

Three successive lieutenant-governors of Ontario – Pauline McGibbon, John Black Aird and Lincoln Alexander – sat on the school's board, and a fourth, Hal Jackman, Toronto's great arts and humanities benefactor, gave a commencement speech at Grenville. I'm sure most of these families had no idea what went on at the school, as the administration monitored our mail and calls and imposed a strict code of secrecy. Even if they had heard rumblings,

The author, right, attended Grenville for the three years starting in 1980.

I don't know if they would have believed them. For some, what happened at Grenville is still too much to swallow.

In 1995, *Maclean's* sent journalist Scott Steele to write a feature story about Grenville. He says the administration provided him with a carefully controlled narrative. Parents used the piece to refute their children's accusations of abuse. Steele later told me how bitterly he regrets being used in this way, and he has apologized to other ex-students for writing the article in the first place. Reading a glossy, flattering magazine story about the school where we'd experienced so much terror compounded the trauma for me and so many other students.

In Grade 8, I was exhausted from the routine. I'd have a full day at school, then cross-country running practice (a rare source of comfort at Grenville). Then there was dinner, dish crew, then homework from 7:00 p.m. into the late evening. One night, I came back late to the tiny room in the trailer where I bunked with three other staff kids. When I found myself last in line for the bathroom, I lay on my top bunk and waited for it to become available. Someone turned the lights off, and I fell asleep. I woke up urinating in my bed. The other boys woke up, and the staff were summoned. They told me I was disgusting and sinful. I was given a choice of being beaten with a two-by-four or sleeping in my own urine until laundry day, which was six days away. I chose the latter. Each day, I had to make my wet and stinking bed, with the other staff kids in the room complaining. By the end of the week I was sick with intense chills, and berated intensely in light-sessions for deliberately becoming sick in order to get attention. I half-believed what the staff were telling me. I thought I must be a terrible person who would burn in hell.

When I was fifteen, under instructions from Mother Judy Sorensen, Grenville staff suddenly moved me to a small, shoddy stone cottage that the school owned in nearby Maitland, where I would live with my parents for the first time in years. In this cold, unpleasant house, I was separated from the student body and endured frequent surprise light-sessions from Farnsworth. At meals, I was forced to sit with staff at a table and subjected to more light-sessions. I even received personal phone calls from the Mothers on Cape Cod. I realized that they all wanted me to become a Brother in the Community of Jesus, and these efforts were designed to "turn me." My mother had enlisted the Mothers and Farnsworth to keep me in the fold.

I refused to let it happen. Shortly after I turned sixteen, and as soon as I was legally able, I left both the Community of Jesus and Grenville forever. I broke with my parents as soon as I could. I had learned that these were all weak people in every way. I had endured their abuse for eight long years, and I was intensely angry. The damage done to me at the Community and Grenville would stay with me my whole life.

My twenties were a decade of precarity and periodic homelessness. I had little contact with either of my parents; my mother remained a devout member of the Community until her death a few years ago. During my stretches of homelessness, I would sleep in the daytime because the night was too dangerous. I did a series of menial jobs to put myself through university, and continued memorizing poetry, passing the five hundred mark of memorized poems at a young age and reading obsessively even when I should have been working. But I found it too difficult – financially and psychologically – to finish school at that time. During this time my birth certificate was stolen by someone with a criminal record who grew up in the cult. My father was trying to protect him. He got a driver's licence under my name with his photo and ran up a criminal record under my name in Alberta where I have never lived. In Ontario he was charged with assault with a deadly weapon under my name but found guilty under his own name. He was never prosecuted for identity theft. As far as I know he may still have ID with my data and his photo that later appeared to be used to cash in a life insurance policy in the state of South Carolina.

I eventually found some stability as a writer and finally sought professional help. The first psychiatrist did not believe my story. He thought I was delusional and told me I was probably schizophrenic. I've always wondered how things might have gone if an adult had tried to help me. Perhaps I might have had a chance for a more stable life. As it is, I've struggled with the long-term effects of complex trauma, as have so many others from the Community and Grenville.

Meanwhile, Grenville continued to abuse children. A Brockville newspaper, *The Recorder and Times*, was ready to publish a story about the abuse in 1989, but it was quashed when the school got wind of it. In 1997, Farnsworth finally retired; he died in 2015 at age eighty-three, denying everything to the end.

It was only in 2007, as rumours of abuse kept surfacing, that the OPP launched an investigation. Many former students reported feeling that the police were not on their side; when the OPP interviewed me, they accused me of lying about my story. In the end, they declined to press criminal charges. "It wasn't in the interest of the public," said Sergeant Kristine Rae in an interview with *The Recorder and Times*. "When you're looking at historical allegations, you're looking at the whole picture."

The damage had been done, however. The school closed its doors in 2007, though it didn't acknowledge the role of the investigation in its decision. "Changing demographics, declining enrolment and increasing operating costs have forced this decision upon us," said then-headmaster Gordon Mintz at the time. (Mintz, meanwhile, had been ordained as an Anglican priest in 2001 and is now a chaplain in the Canadian Armed Forces.) The public exposure also encouraged hundreds of students to come together on a now-defunct website called FACTNet, established as a forum for survivors from American cults to relate their experiences. It was incredibly cathartic, the first time many of us had spoken to others who had suffered at Grenville and the Community.

Our story finally reached the public eye. Some students, and some with considerable resources, retained a legal team, formed a class of 1,360 ex-students – including me – and launched a civil class-action suit. Named in the claim were the school and the estates of Al Haig and Charles Farnsworth.

In September 2019, after twelve long years of litigation, the class-action trial commenced in Ontario's Superior Court of Justice. Our legal team argued that the defendants were systemically negligent and breached the duty of care and fiduciary duty it owed its students. We sought $200 million in compensation, along with $25 million in punitive damages. I sat in court for much of the five weeks with a rotating group of former students. We were there not only to bear witness to horrors past, but to make the case for the past's insistent, debilitating and at times unendurable effect on our present lives.

The five weeks of trial revealed many instances of abuse, as well as an intense focus on sexual sins exquisitely tailored to destroy the natural sexual and emotional development of the pubescent teen. Andersen and Sorensen, unbeknownst to all of us at the Community, were lovers who nevertheless railed against homosexuality, saying they could "feel it in the Spirit" if a gay person walked onto the property. As a former member and United Church minister wrote in a sworn statement, the Mothers were so obsessed with what they considered deviant sexual practices that they forbade married couples from engaging in oral sex.

Cay Andersen and Judy Sorensen, Grenville yearbook, 1980s.

Always in mimetic rivalry, Farnsworth took the Mothers' Christian sexual repression and guilt complex to an extreme level, preying sexually on students himself. One student, a staff child who was born at the school, recounted that Farnsworth constantly slut-shamed her and quizzed her on her sexual fantasies. Another former student testified how, after a classmate reported that the witness was gay, Farnsworth held twenty counselling sessions with him, calling him satanic and interrogating him about his sexuality. "I started to form this understanding in my mind that I was worse than a killer, and I was definitely going to hell," he said. When the boy admitted that two neighbours had molested him as a child, Farnsworth was fascinated: "He wanted to know the age of the men who molested me, how frequently I was molested, where it occurred, what kind of sexual abuse. He wanted details." Farnsworth informed the student that even as a young kid he had Satan in him – that he'd been running around all summer long in a Speedo, tempting these men to touch him. That Satan had a firm hold of this student even then, using this boy as temptation, a tool of evil. It wasn't the fault of these men.

One paying student, Bradley Merson, told me about being light-sessioned several times by Farnsworth while naked. Another student testified that Farnsworth ran his hand up his leg and touched his penis. Students described being injured and traumatized from excessive paddling. Once, when I was in Grade 7, Farnsworth saw me looking down a hallway – I think I had forgotten something. He accused me of having sexual thoughts toward the girls who were standing there. I was shocked and horribly ashamed to be accused of those things. I had not gone through puberty yet.

The legal team for Grenville and the estates of Farnsworth and Haig denied our claims in court. They argued that punishments were never abusive or imposed without justification. Furthermore, they insisted, Farnsworth did not foster an atmosphere of fear or intimidation, or isolate students from their families. The defendants also categorically denied that there was any "systemic campaign to promote and indoctrinate students in the teachings and practices of the Community of Jesus." When *Toronto Life* wrote to the Community for response, their lawyer said that the lawsuit did not allege any wrongful conduct by the Community of Jesus or by anyone there. "The conduct that the author apparently alleges is said to have taken place some 700 miles from the Community of Jesus nearly 50 years ago," he wrote. "No fair-minded person could expect comment about allegations about things that are said to have occurred a half-century ago in another country."

The judgment finally came in February 2020. In her decision, Justice Janet Leiper clearly identified Grenville's mission: to enforce on its students a way of living, using Community of Jesus practices, including violence, shame and humiliation for students who were insufficiently obedient, too haughty or too proud. She found that Grenville failed to meet the standard of care and ruled in the plaintiffs' favour on every count. Her final analysis is damning: "I have concluded that the evidence of maltreatment and the varieties of abuse perpetrated on students' bodies and minds in the name of the COJ [Community of Jesus] values of submission and obedience was class-wide and decades-wide." Her judgment would be followed by a separate trial for damages, although the defendants appealed the ruling. The original ruling was later upheld unanimously by a panel of three judges.

Grenville may be closed and dismantled, and the students finally granted their day in court, but the Community of Jesus in Cape Cod continues to operate. As late as 2000, Community leaders were writing to Grenville staff. Farnsworth, under the spiritual authority of Andersen and Sorensen, learned to follow their lead, surrounding himself with legitimators, acolytes, powerful patrons and supporters who would ensure he could do whatever he wanted.

Farnsworth's son, Donald, who at the time of writing was undertaking a divinity degree at Wycliffe College at the University of

Toronto, objected to Justice Leiper's decision. In conversations with *Toronto Life*'s fact-checking department, he said he had a fantastic time as a student at Grenville; he played basketball, ran track, acted in school plays. He acknowledged that Grenville was strict – he even admits that he once got the paddle – but he said that discipline helped him become a confident human being, and to acknowledge Jesus as his saviour. The same was true of the work-jobs, he said. The school had farm animals for a time, and Donald often had to wake up early to clean the barns. "It was quite a good experience for us to learn the value of manual labour," he said. He admitted his father was "an authoritarian," but insisted that he followed God and looked after the best interests of students and staff.

He disputes the abuse allegations, even though there were more than 1,300 plaintiffs. "Every single one of those allegations, when they claimed abusive behaviour, they were either embellished or totally made up," he said. "And how do I know this? Because I was there. I was there the whole time." He said the judge simply took the defendants' word for what happened without external corroboration, and that most students would say they had a positive experience. Of the others – the "squeaky wheels," as he calls them – he said, "This group had a few ringleaders with issues. And they might have had a terrible time at Grenville. Maybe we weren't the right place for them. I don't think we did anything to damage them, and we certainly didn't do it intentionally."

Our brief day in court was enormously important. For me, the testimony of the expert witness, a psychologist and former psychology professor, about the degree of damage Grenville's abuse caused, was an epiphany of sorts. That day, the courtroom was well attended by former students, some of whom had flown in from across the country. Many were suddenly crying. Several had to leave the courtroom. For the first time, these former students heard someone in authority recognize that their suffering was real. For the first time, our voices were heard and believed.

The Origins of the Community of Jesus

1. The Early Years

How did this sect start? How did they come up with such an idea? What were the circumstances that allowed it to get started? What let it get so out of control? How did those in control justify their abusive behaviour?

In the 1990s, respected professor Dr. Ronald M. Enroth wrote a chapter about the Community of Jesus in his well-known book *Churches that Abuse* (Zondervan, 1993), in which he positions the Community of Jesus this way:

> Two laypersons, Cay Andersen and Judy Sorensen, founded the Community around 1970 (Mrs. Andersen died several years ago). They soon became affectionately known as "Mother Cay" and "Mother Judy," and were at the center of the controversy that has swirled around the organization in recent years. In addition to what one churchman called its "lack of ecclesiology," the COJ has been accused of promoting a "theology of control" that focuses on attitudinal sins like jealousy, rebellion, willfulness, haughtiness, and idolatry. Critics and former members have argued that the Community has shifted toward an unbalanced, unbiblical, and highly structured program resulting in some people being abused emotionally and spiritually. There have also been reports of some forms of physical abuse. Media accounts, including an extensive article in *Boston* magazine,

have raised suspicions. These have been denounced by the COJ leadership. (152–53)

Cay Andersen and Judy Sorensen claimed to have first met each other at the Church of the Holy Spirit in Orleans, Massachusetts, in 1958. At this time Cay Andersen was running a seasonal bed and breakfast with her husband, Bill, (and her teenage son, Peter) called Rock Harbor Manor, overlooking Rock Harbor and Cape Cod Bay. Judy Sorensen was staying in her five-bedroom summer home on nearby Crystal Lake with her husband, also named Bill, and their four children. According to some of their children and others close to them, there was an immediate and very strong attraction between them.

Church of the Holy Spirit in Orleans. Courtesy Ewan Whyte.

Peter Andersen, Cay's son, explained their early days together in an interview when I visited him in Europe:

> They met at the Church of the Holy Spirit in Orleans. And the history before it is that my mother had been very sick. We moved from our house in North Eastham and bought the Rock Harbor Manor from a wealthy man who lived in

Brewster, and Cay ran a B and B the whole summer, and she overdid it and she became quite ill by the end of the summer. She had epilepsy seizures, and hepatitis B . . . A friend of hers, the doctor's wife from East Ham, invited her to the healing services at the old Church of the Holy Spirit in Orleans, Cape Cod. And they were every Thursday. That was common in the Episcopal Church in those days. And that's where she met Judy. According to their account, in later years, the physical attraction was immediate. And I think, Cay, when Cay went over to Judy's house, and realized how wealthy Judy was, I think that was a big draw as well. Judy's husband was the president or vice-president of Key Light Chemicals in California, which had been started by . . . Bill Sorensen's father, and he was making probably sixty thousand a year back in, you know, 1956, 1957, '58. It was a fortune back then. So . . . she was always coming home and talking – "Oh, Mrs. Sorensen has such beautiful, beautiful things, and she's so rich" – anyway, the two fell in love. My parents' marriage wasn't very good, and we eventually moved to Crystal Lake. I used to go there after school.

The two women's secret affair appears to have started immediately and they often travelled together for the next few years to somewhat conservative and often very fringe religious gatherings to meet and hear Christian speakers, all while publicly having very hostile views on gays and lesbians.

Peter Andersen continued:

Cay was often going to where they lived in Short Hills, New Jersey, and she and Judy would go travel throughout the United States and speak to church groups and different Charismatic churches or Pentecostal churches, which was fine with my dad and me, because my mother was so explosive in her temperament that we were glad that she was gone. But more and more the relationship developed and Judy finally decided, in 1961 maybe, that the Sorensens would move to their house in Crystal Lake, which they did. My father first had to renovate the Crystal Lake house to winterize it. It was a three-season home on the lake. And during the time when they were winterizing it, our two families lived together at Rock Harbor. And that's how this whole concept of the families living together came about. So we all moved back to Crystal Lake, and this was perfect for them because they could leave and go on their ministry trips and not have to worry about the kids because my father was there as a parental figure. Bill Sorenson, in the meantime, had left his job and was working in some job in the Boston area.

Cay Andersen was born Carrie May Whitcomb in Weymouth, Massachusetts, in 1913. She grew up with a non-religious mother who was very strict with her. Cay would complain many years later about frequent corporal punishment and would often say as an adult, "I never thought my mother loved me." She completed high school and took some courses at a local community college. She married Bill Andersen, who had a small construction company, and eventually she ran Rock Harbor Manor, a seasonal bed and breakfast. She was not particularly religious but maintained an interest in Christian Science for a number of years before she met Judy Sorensen.

Judy Sorensen, born Julanne Hales in 1928 in Texas, was the love child of a very wealthy Texas oil tycoon whom she never met. She was raised in New Jersey by her non-religious maternal grandmother. She finished high school and started some courses at UCLA. She was a heavy drinker even when she was young – her nickname was "Jolly Judy" when she was drinking. She first met Bill Sorensen at a party of UCLA students. The story goes that she was attracted to him immediately because of his gabardine pants (apparently a display of financial means at the time). Bill's family was very wealthy. He quickly became vice-president of Key Light Chemicals, a company owned by his father. She married him and they lived first in Los Angeles, then in the very wealthy suburb of Short Hills, New Jersey. She was not religious but was converted by her neighbour Mildred, a Baptist who was married to a successful doctor. Judy's husband built a house beside Mildred's summer home on Crystal Lake so they could spend more time in the summers together.

In 1961 Judy and her husband, Bill, sold their winter home in Short Hills and moved full time to Cape Cod. The Sorensens were now across the town from the Andersens.

By this time Judy Sorensen was an avid follower – and for a while, a close acolyte – of the very controversial protestant Christian faith healer and speaker Agnes Sanford (1897–1982), who is often considered to be the founder of the now largely debunked "Inner Healing Movement." Sanford was the daughter of Presbyterian missionaries in China where she grew up in a fundamentalist setting before going to the U.S. for college. She took a teaching certificate for the state of North Carolina but did not earn a degree. She then developed her own seemingly idiosyncratic memory-healing ideas. She was a popular figure in the lead-up to the Charismatic Renewal of the 1960s, though there is now a considerable amount of dispute with her once relatively well-known ideas.

In 1958, the year Cay and Judy met, Sanford founded the Agnes Sanford School of Pastoral Care in New Hampshire. Judy, already a close follower, would visit her in New Hampshire and started taking Cay on her visits.

Many people have had trouble with Sanford's approach. Of the several concerns, a key one was the idea of a charismatic leader who presents themselves as an authority because of having a special understanding of God. That said, given the time in America, it is not surprising that she did find a considerable number of followers.

The following passage from Sanford's book *Sealed Orders* shows how her ideas of Jesus were entirely personal and unrelated to any accepted Christian approach: "I 'laid on the table' all my preconceived ideas and paid no attention to what anyone said except Jesus – not the Bible nor St. Paul nor my husband nor anyone" (102–3).

Here is an example of her beliefs about healing:

[The] beautiful young wife [of a missionary] stood up to give thanks that God had healed her spirit after long darkness. [. . .] Some months later she hanged herself from her bedroom window after trying to cut her wrists. She [. . .] did not die for several days, during which time the missionaries besought her to confess her sins . . . poor dear. [. . .]

It would have been so easy to heal this lovely lady, even as I long afterward was healed. If only some one of God's ministers had known that he himself was a channel for God's power and had laid his hands on her and prayed for the love of Jesus to come into her and lift her out of darkness into His light! (Sanford, 48)

This attitude to healing is similar to one that we find a little later in the preaching/teaching of Andersen and Sorensen and their Community of Jesus. The idea that the two women could successfully command God to do something is in much of their preaching. At times it was as though they were directly playing God. During arguments and screaming matches with each other they would often say to close outsiders, whether Sisters or members, "We are fighting over the body of Christ."

Sanford was the first real spiritual teacher of Andersen and

Sorensen, and they started on their faith-healing and sect-founding journey by imitating her. Before and during this time they also both claimed to be interested in the work of Emmet Fox. But it appears this interest was more in the interpretation of Fox by Sanford, who wrote in her autobiography, "Then someone gave me a copy of Emmet Fox's *The Sermon on the Mount*, and although the language of this book was not that to which I was accustomed, speaking of 'treating' and 'demonstrating' when I would have said 'praying' and 'receiving answers to prayer,' still it thrilled my soul because it made clear to me the reality of the spiritual body that interpenetrates the physical body, and of the spiritual world in which we really live. This book is based strongly and squarely on the words that Jesus actually said" (Sanford, 103).

This idea has been pointed out by Dr. Jane Gumprecht in her book *Abusing Memory*, which is about Agnes Sanford, as completely wrong. In *Sermon on the Mount*, Fox writes:

> What did Jesus teach?
> ... The plain fact is Jesus taught no theology whatever. His teaching is entirely spiritual or metaphysical. ... All the doctrines and theologies of the churches are human inventions ... Men built up absurd and very horrible fables about a limited and man-like God who conducted his universe very much as an ignorant and barbarous prince ... Then a farfetched and very inconsistent legend was built up concerning original sin, vicarious blood atonement, infinite punishment for finite transgressions ... Now, no such theory as this is taught in the Bible. ...
>
> The "Plan of Salvation" which figured so prominently in the evangelical sermons and divinity books of a past generation is as completely unknown to the Bible as it is to the Koran. (2–5)

Obviously, Emmet Fox was not in line with most typical mainline Christian doctrine of the time. Dr. Jane Gumprecht writes from a Christian perspective on the same passage: "This passage speaks for itself. From it we can say with confidence Emmet Fox did not hold to Christian doctrine. Yet in three different chapters in *Sealed Orders* and *Healing Touch of God* Sanford pays tribute to him as the most important source for her 'prayer of faith' and Inner Healing" (34).

Fox is also very far away from the authoritarian path Andersen and Sorensen were about to take. In fact it is difficult to square Emmet Fox's ideas with any of their teaching and preaching. It is Sanford who was the close mentor and teacher of Judy Sorensen, then Cay Andersen. They would copy Sanford and, like her, see no boundaries on where their inspired invention could take them. They started to counsel people about more serious life concerns and problems despite having no formal training.

Sorensen even copied the style, pacing and diction of Sanford in much of her public speaking. If you listen to Sanford's "Healing of Memories" preaching recording, which is now public on YouTube, then listen to a recording of Sorensen in her also readily available preaching recordings, the similarity is remarkable.

However, slowly, from roughly 1964 to 1965, Cay and Judy became increasingly interested in even more extreme people and groups than the already fringe Sanford. They had a successful preaching circuit with the more mainstream, by comparison, Faith at Work conferences in the early and mid-1960s, as well as their own independent touring, preaching and faith-healing circuit with stop-offs at a significant number of Pentecostal churches, as well as many evangelical-leaning mainline churches, both locally and throughout the United States Midwest and South. Two more mainline-leaning ones were Parkminster Presbyterian in Rochester, New York, and Stanwich Congregational Church in Greenwich, Connecticut, under Pastor Nate Adams, who was a strong supporter of their work, according to Rockefeller heiress Isabel Lincoln Elmer in her book *Cinderella Rockefeller*. Through him, Isabel Lincoln Elmer became a follower and appears to have been one of their biggest catches. She describes her religious experience with the two women in March 1966 at a "Faith at Work" meeting like this:

> And then I sensed their presence in front of me, and I looked up and saw their smiling faces. "What do you want?" Judy gently asked me.
> "I would like to be able to heal people like you can," I stammered.
> Then they calmly laid their hands on my head, and told me to just thank Jesus, as they prayed. They started to pray, so quietly that not even the person sitting next to me could hear them. Something – I can only describe it as like electricity – surged through my body. Everything inside of me seemed to sink to the floor, and then soar up into space. I burst into tears and started sobbing, not for sorrow, but for joy. I was filled with an exhilaration totally unknown to me, and I felt like shouting and laughing and crying all at once. I felt I had given everything to Jesus, and He was mine, and I was His, completely and forever. (173)

I remember seeing Isabel Lincoln Elmer many times and speaking with her at the Community of Jesus compound. She was treated as a celebrity. Elmer's mother was described in her book by a quote from a news article in 1925 as "one of the important heiresses of American society." I remember the reverence with which she was addressed and the red-carpet treatment she would receive. I understood that she was perceived to possess more humanity and value than the poorer people, especially the poorer children like me.

She describes another one of her early experiences (around 1966) with Andersen and Sorensen that some former members would consider to be an episode of grooming:

> One of the young women came out on the manor's front terrace and said, "Bel, Cay and Judy would like to see you now."
> With heart pounding, I followed her to a little room attached to the garage, where they did their counseling. As soon as I saw their smiling faces, I burst into tears. I felt as if my heart would break.
> "That's all right, Bel," Cay said. "Don't try to bottle it all up."
> So I kept on crying. At last, my sobs subsided, and I blurted out, "Oh, Cay and Judy, I need help! Please help me!"
> They both looked at me lovingly, and Judy said, "We've been waiting a long time to hear that, Bel. We'd love to help you. But we couldn't before, because you hadn't asked. Now is the time. We have much we think God has given us to say to you." (187)

According to family members and those close to them, the two women were very interested in wealth and the lifestyle that it brought. Some Pentecostals especially at the time had issues with Andersen and Sorensen over their fancy upscale clothes, expensive jewellery, makeup and lipstick, but they were a niche success. They went on expensive trips, had a brand-new Mercedes and an Amphicar – a kind of car that was instantly transferable into a boat. They collected hundreds of thousands of dollars in estate jewellery and revelled in luxury. Yet the following is Elmer's account of her conversation with Cay and Judy about her wealth and being a member of the Rockefeller family:

Cay said, "I read something recently about wealthy families and the collective resentment that comes against them, and it makes a lot of sense. I've no idea whether your ancestors' business dealings were ethical, but there must be a great deal of residual bitterness against them and the whole Rockefeller family. You know the Bible says that the sins of the fathers are visited on the children down to the third and fourth generation, and all of it has piled on your generation's shoulders."

My heart quickened; Cay was getting at something that had troubled me all my life. (187)

By 1966 Andersen and Sorensen were notable players in the travelling preaching circuit, receiving substantial donations and notoriety, while enjoying an extravagant lifestyle. They interacted with Harald Bredesen who influenced Pat Robertson and Pat Boone and had connections with the often considered charlatan, Norman Vincent Peale, the author of *The Power of Positive Thinking*. Al Haig, the future abusive headmaster of Grenville Christian College, was, in the 1960s, an associate pastor to Peale at Marble Collegiate Church in New York, and is said to have exclaimed to Harald Bredesen's wife, "I just love your husband," to which she replied, "You don't have to live with him."

Andersen's and Sorensen's knowledge of biblical Christianity was limited from many accounts. Even their own preaching tapes show this, with Sorensen being recorded asking about passages that fit into what her ideas were. But in these groups it hardly mattered. It was all about sounding taken over by the Spirit and having "God" speak through them, receiving donations and attempting to heal evangelicals.

They were constantly looking for other opportunities to preach and Christian groups to meet and solicit donations from for their preaching tours. Cay Andersen's son, Peter, seriously doubted that they were even Christian at all.

2. The Evangelical Sisterhood of Mary

Andersen and Sorensen made a special trip to Toronto, Ontario, in the winter of 1965 to meet self-styled Mother Basilea, Klara Schlink, who was having an unsuccessful tour of North America at the time. These eager Americans were welcome company and Mother Basilea told them about her sect the Evangelical Sisterhood of Mary, which was also sometimes called Kanaan, that she ran with her co-leader self-styled Mother Martyria. Founded in 1947, the Sisterhood had its own large compound with a substantial area of land in Darmstadt, Germany, and functioned, according to Basilea, like an ancient religious convent/monastic order with even a mini-farm on the property. They claimed to be influenced by Lutheran doctrine but had much more in common with more extreme American Pentecostals. Many Germans were still collectively grieving under the shame and guilt of the Second World War and the horror of having enabled the Holocaust. With their own extensive and substantial donations the Sisterhood opened a small rest house in Jerusalem, where they presented themselves as helping Jewish people who had survived the Holocaust. Despite their protests to the contrary, they were also interested (according to former members) in converting people.

The Evangelical Sisterhood of Mary was outwardly consumed with Israel, while failing to notice that their own leadership was, according to some former members, both racist and anti-Semitic themselves. Andersen and Sorensen were also well known to be racist. Cay's son, Peter, stated: "Before meeting Basilea [of the Evangelical Sisterhood of Mary] they were involved with the granddaughter of A.J. Gordon who was into the pyramids and a very racist organization (at the time) called Anglo-Israelism as well as a couple of charismatic ladies in the Midwest of the United States who claimed that they were sinless and had received their resurrection bodies already, and published these very cheap newspapers where there were prophecies about the most bizarre topics.

They claimed there were termites living on the moon, huge termites which ate moondust. So they had a pretty bizarre background."

Peter added that Cay hated Abraham Lincoln because he "freed the slaves," as they were better off before Emancipation. One affidavit discusses Judy telling a rare Black visitor that "he should be with his kind." In my time at the Community, I was a witness to both leaders' racist views.

The three women connected easily in Toronto and it was decided that Andersen and Sorensen would go to visit the Evangelical Sisterhood of Mary (ESM) compound in Darmstadt in the spring of 1965. That visit went so well they went for a second visit a few months later in the summer. In 1966 the co-leader of the ESM, Mother Martyria, visited Hartford, Connecticut, and then, along with two other Sisters of Mary, visited Andersen and Sorensen at Rock Harbor Manor on Cape Cod to see where the two women had thought of starting their own sect, following the approach of the ESM in Germany.

Former members of the Evangelical Sisterhood say it was well known in the community that German Methodist pastor Paul Riedinger randomly decided to start calling Basilea and Martyria by the titles "Mothers." He later became involved in the New Apostolic Church and started dressing up in his own elaborately fashioned robes to the extent that even the Sisters at the ESM found it strange.

One former member of the Evangelical Sisterhood of Mary who knew the American visitors during their time there explained the Sisterhood as a business, a "high-powered sales organization promoting their product which is Mother Basilea Schlink and her books." As a result, this member said, "Cay and Judy received the traditional love-bombing from the Sisters, praised them and made a fuss over them and they became more and more involved. The Sisters were hoping to establish a base in the United States which they did in Phoenix [Arizona] and Cay and Judy became closer and closer to the Mothers [in Darmstadt] until they had this great split back in 1969."

Peter Andersen described the falling-out between them:

> Mother Martyria spent about four weeks with Cay teaching her how to run a Sisterhood and that was in the fall of 1968, I believe. They had this big blow-up in mid-1968, which is when Judy went to Darmstadt, to Kanaan, as they called it. And Mother Basilea went to train Cay on how to run a Sisterhood, and when I say "run" I mean the "light fellowships," which were brutal. One of the Sisters from the Sisterhood [the Community of Jesus was originally called "The Little Sisters of Mary"] that was founded in Rock Harbor with Mother Basilea's help, had a romantic affair with Judy and Cay became fanatically jealous of the two of them. This was a horrible, explosive situation at Rock Harbor and it was through Judy going to Darmstadt that things calmed down; later that Sister, who was American, went to Darmstadt as well and became a Sister of Mary. She really played up to Mother Basilea. She was a climber and she wanted to be the top and she got there really quickly. She was a praiser of Mother Basilea's right from the start, an admirer and very vocal about it.

The primary method of control that passed from the Evangelical Sisterhood of Mary to the Community of Jesus was their "Lichtgemeinschaften." Translated literally, these are "fellowships/communities in the light" meetings, or as the Germans simplified it for the Americans, "light-sessions."

These "fellowships in the light" were based on the Sisters' modern interpretation of the practices of Medieval Catholic religious groups known as "The Chapter" or "Chapter of Faults" in a few Catholic religious orders. The French abbey of Cluny, founded in

910, appears to be the first record we have of some kind of (vague) general confessing ritual. It claims the practice began before the year 1000. In the early years of the Sisters of Mary they copied the name of the original medieval term, calling their own gatherings "Chapter Meetings" and the room for which these meetings took place at the ESM was called "The Chapter Hall." This was done with only an imagined understanding of what these ancient rituals were.

In her 1945 Circular Letter, Mother Basilea wrote: "This open confession of sin was something which God worked amongst us, in Falkengesaess (at a retreat) and subsequently at each Wednesday meeting. We admitted our sins in front of the whole group and in fact under the discipline of the Spirit, we specifically confessed those sins which humbled us the most" (quoted in Jansson and Lemmetyinen, *When the Walls Came Tumbling Down*, trans. Jeannie Dobney).

Light-sessions were supposedly an evangelical and extreme attempt to live a Christian life according to the Bible passage in the New Testament, 1 John 1:6–7: "If we claim to be sharing in His life while we walk in the dark, our words and our lives are a lie; but if we walk in the light as he himself is in the light, then we share together a common life, and we are being cleansed from every sin by the blood of Jesus his Son."

Mother Basilea had a PhD in psychology and seems to have used her knowledge to considerable effect. The website of the Evangelical Sisterhood of Mary states: "God commissioned our two spiritual mothers to build a chapel where he would receive honour and worship. As confirmation they received the following scripture: 'Let them make me a sanctuary that I may dwell among them' (Exodus 25:8)."

According to former members, the Mothers would open the Bible at random and take a prophecy from reading a random line of text. But if they didn't get the answer they wanted they would covertly keep trying until they got the answer they desired.

Here are excerpts from a piece originally written in German and published in 2007 (under the title *Eine ehemalige Marienschwester erzählt ihre Geschichte*) by Charlene Andersen about light-sessions during her fourteen years as a member of the Evangelical Sisterhood of Mary in Darmstadt (she left in 1999):

> And this is how the "Lichtgemeinschaften" were carried out: one Sister after another had to confess which of their own words and deeds had harmed the community. While she was standing there, everybody who found something sinful in the standing Sister, was invited to speak . . .
>
> During these meetings it was not allowed to justify oneself. One had to act quietly and subservient and to humiliate oneself . . . I think the terrors of these meetings I have never overcome.

Community of Jesus light-sessions began with members who were confronted by Community members who pointed out their sins in a very confrontational, methodical and highly processed way. The person being light-sessioned was not allowed to speak and several other members would engage in "wolf-packing" them, as former Community of Jesus elite member David Manuel states, in the most hurtful and psychologically abusive way. In these meetings those being light-sessioned were often forced to admit to previous sins or emotional wounds – often imaginary or entirely made up – that were then used to get the person enduring the light-session (sometimes even months or years later) to submit to authority. This was almost always followed up by a collective "love-bombing." This love-bombing after submission was very important, as the emotionally raw, light-sessioned individual was vulnerable to attestations of care and love at this moment. The person light-sessioned was told how much they were loved by the same people who had just been emotionally abusing them moments before. They were told that the people in the outside world don't have real friends like their friends in the Community of Jesus. I do not know of a single counselling professional taking part in any of these meetings. This was entirely amateur and done as the leading members felt inspired or led by "the Spirit."

New members would be slowly and gently eased into this lifestyle until they were hooked. Then their light-sessions would be much harsher and in line with how the Community actually lives. Many members seemed to become emotionally addicted to these light-sessions. As former teacher at Grenville and Community of Jesus member Joan Childs said in an interview with the news program *W5*, "This was our way of life." At the Community of Jesus, light-sessions could come at any time; they were unrelenting. In recent years the Community of Jesus has dropped the use of the word/term "light-session," but former members who have left recently say they are still going on, some with the same level of intensity as when they were the subject of criticism by *Chronicle*, a Boston television news documentary in 1993.

I was addressed with the ferocity and intensity of a light-session by a long-term Community member I had known as a child there with witnesses present while visiting the compound (that has since banned me) within the last few years. It was clear to me from this experience, and from my extensive interviewing of many members who have recently left, that this practice of light-sessions still goes on, even if the term is no longer openly used.

When I was a child at the Community of Jesus starting at age eight, the light-sessions were terrifying. They were often accompanied by violence and always held the threat of violence. These forced public confessions of guilt – of things that were often unintelligible to a child – imitated the Catholic confession style, with the adults playing the roles of the God-inspired priests by granting the forgiveness of God after punishments to the children for the most minor of infractions. When there were no infractions, which was often, some were made up. This was all made worse by almost all children being separated from their parents, as was the general practice. I was forbidden to speak with my parents, even though I was only eight years old. The children of the very wealthy were the only children I remember being allowed to live with their parents when I was there.

The patterns of authoritarian control at the Evangelical Sisterhood of Mary were copied at the Community of Jesus and later Grenville, and were more extreme in the United States, due to the personality issues of Community of Jesus leaders. A former member of the Evangelical Sisterhood stated that Mother Basilea told Andersen and Sorensen that they should not run a monastic community with children. Basilea also disapproved of light-sessions on children. But the two American women disagreed.

It was on the basis of this very harsh, light-session–focused lifestyle that the Community of Jesus was organized and controlled. Its leaders managed to lead lives of luxury with a private plane and an estate in Bermuda, while so many of those of the low ranks and young children suffered.

After cementing close links to Grenville Christian College in the 1970s, the same light-sessions were learned and used on unsuspecting paying students at Grenville Christian College near Brockville, Ontario, from 1973 to 1997, according to the legal ruling, but they seem to have carried on much longer from former student accounts. Mother Betty, who gained control from Mother Judy of the Community of Jesus as its sole leader, wrote a letter to staff reminding them of their vows of obedience to the leaders of the Community of Jesus in the early 2000s. All staff when I was there as a student in the 1980s were members of the Community of Jesus.

Peter Andersen explained that both Mother Basilea and Mother Martyria "spent months at Rock Harbor on Cape Cod to teach

Cay and Judy how to set up a monastic community and most importantly, how to perform light-sessions, which they called a 'Monastic Discipline.'" Cay and Judy's version was brutal beyond what was practised in Germany. Later, Charles Farnsworth, under Cay and Judy's influence, imported them to use on children at Grenville. The institutional foundations are from the practices of that order in Germany, and Peter also noted that Basilea was influenced by her parents, who were understood by former members to be ardent National Socialists during the Second World War:

Peter Andersen with Mother Basilea, 1968.

In January of 1968 Mother Basilea stayed at Rock Harbor with Cay and Judy. The purpose of the visit was to indoctrinate Cay and Judy into the secret teachings and doctrines of the Sisters of Mary. One of the Sisters of Mary had received inner visions about Mother Basilea's greatness and her primacy in the history of the Church and the world. I was asked at one point to translate these for Mother Basilea's visit. But I was removed from the task suddenly after some doubts I raised about such prophecies.

Mother Basilea wrote me from Rock Harbor during her stay. It was during this time that Cay and Judy, together with Mother Basilea, founded the Sisterhood at Rock Harbor, calling themselves "The little Sisters of Mary." They were featured in the next newsletter of the Sisterhood of Mary in Darmstadt with a write-up and photographs.

Postcard, 1968.   Mother Basilia writing to Peter Anderson, 1968.

After the dramatic breach with the Sisterhood of Mary in 1969, Cay and Judy renamed their community the "Sisters of the Community of Jesus." Judy went in the summer of 1968 to live on "Kanaan," the large estate of the Sisters of Mary.

In the autumn of that same year, while Judy was still in Darmstadt, Mother Martyria went to Rock Harbor to spend several weeks with Cay to instruct her further in the art of "Light Fellowships" and the discipline of the Sisters. Cay and Judy later took these sessions to a whole new level, constantly inflicting them upon vulnerable children and young people.

Of course the Mothers, on both sides of the pond, never came under such criticism.

Several former members have written accounts of their time in the Evangelical Sisterhood. Their philosophy, at first, appears to be a kind of sin-drenched make-it-up-as-you-go kind of ragtag thing, seeming much closer to extreme American puritanical evangelical Protestantism (Pentecostal), rather than contemporaneous mainstream European Protestant traditions. A closer look reveals that it is a much darker actual micro-totalitarian control.

According to Marianne Jansson and Riitta Lemmetyinen in their academic work and later in *Wenn Mauern fallen* (translated into English as *When the Walls Came Tumbling Down*), former members explained that "'Fellowships in Light' provide the framework for the concrete expression of repentance. It is here that sins that have affected other members of the community are openly confessed and forgiveness for them is proclaimed. The sisterly ministry of admonishing one another over unrecognized guilt is also performed here. It is the site where God drills into the hearts of the Sisters until tears of contrition flow. This is the source of the reconciliation that is the secret of Canaan [the ESM in Germany]."

Another former member of the Sisterhood was recorded in *Wenn Mauern fallen* stating, "Mother Basilea knew that we shuddered at the thought. We know that – understandably – many fear 'Fellowships in Light.' However, in spite of the fear, one can still thank Jesus for them: 'Even if it hurts me and I find it difficult I want to love "Fellowships in Light" because I know that the truth makes me free.'"

The authors later asked, "What are the consequences of the 'Fellowship in Light' for Sister X? A nervous breakdown?" They noted that "Mother Basilea teaches that no Sister of Mary will be spared such an experience. God will choose a time to deal with her through His chosen instruments. She encounters Him as the God of Wrath who is completely holy and recognises through the encounter that she is but a 'vessel of sin.' God deals the sinner a 'blow of death' to annihilate her 'selfhood'" (Jansson and Lemmetyinen, 45).

However, according to Mother Basilea the sessions were to lead toward spiritual healing and not a breakdown: "We become spiritually healthy when we are broken. This is precisely the opposite of what our intellect tells us. We think: 'If I had to experience something like that I will be spiritually broken.' But the reality is that I become spiritually whole because it is God's action in my life" (Jansson and Lemmetyinen, 45).

At the Community of Jesus, light-sessions were often savage – as has been publicly stated by many ex-members. They could happen at any time and for any reason. They were usually off the cuff and sudden, seemingly coming out of nowhere. There were also organized and scheduled light-sessions, which were so emotionally upsetting as a young child being ganged up on by several adults that children often would, over time, lose a sense of their inner selves, as I did.

When I attended Grenville, the staff, who were at that time all members of the Community of Jesus, sometimes scheduled them as "light-groups" with each other and with non-resident members of the Community, following the Community of Jesus practice. The travesty is that at Grenville the mostly emotionally damaged staff freely exercised them on unsuspecting students who would have had no previous understanding of the practice and experienced it for what it was: severely abusive mind control. The students, being very young, would have had no way of fighting back and would usually just internalize it.

Interestingly, Jansson and Lemmetyinen recorded one of the lower ranking Sisters of Mary stating this in the 1990s, when they would be completely unaware of the Community of Jesus and Grenville Christian College: "Some friends of the community have attempted to imitate the practice of 'Fellowships in Light,' however sooner or later most of those attempts have failed. The fact that only the Sisters of Mary can actually maintain this practice of open confession of sin, only serves to increase the admiration of the friends" (38).

This begs the question: How many others might there have been?

In the Sisters of Mary, a large Fellowship in Light could take four or five hours or even more. Transgressions identified in the small Fellowships in Light and that have been judged to be serious or recurrent may also have to be confessed again in the large Fellowships in Light. Of course, the sins are often illusory, as is captured in this passage from *Wenn Mauern fallen*:

> "But what if something that is obviously unjustified is said to me?" I asked the Sister assigned as my councillor.
> "Accept the censure in silence and pray until you recognize that it is your fault if you cannot accept a reprimand. Jesus also endured unjust accusation and he remained silent." (41)

This sounds so similar to the Community and Grenville, and is reminiscent of Orwell's famous dystopian novel *1984* about totalitarian regimes.

Over time the sessions became addictive to many of the members, especially those with troubled backgrounds, which appeared to be most members.

Peter Andersen shared this insight about light-sessions: "Almost every strong thing, say, a beautiful sunset, can release endorphins. Well, these light-sessions, they're so bad and they're so painful, your body produces endorphins to counteract that, and you think it's a spiritual experience and that God is closer to you because of it."

I have found this to be one of the most accurate descriptions of the emotional links between perceived spiritual experience and light-sessions. These light-sessions can, especially over time, make people feel like they are close to God. My mother was a very devout member of the Community of Jesus. In extensive recorded interviews with me toward the end of her life, she described being light-sessioned at the Community of Jesus as being very close to God, as an experience of God.

Former ESM members talk about Basilea being influenced by

some chaplains in a meeting in Bavaria before the war, who practised a variation of the rites. But they would have all been aware of the "total honesty" group meetings with their large-scale public confessions of sin, started by the very controversial Frank Buchman (1878–1961) and his First Christian Century group, which he founded in 1921. The name later changed to the Oxford Group in 1928, and changed yet again in 1938 to Moral Re-Armament. Buchman had a considerable following both in the U.S. and in Europe. Some of his group meetings and/or "house parties," as they were misleadingly called, included "total honesty," a kind of full disclosure that is still popular with various addiction groups, especially sex addiction, today.

Buchman believed that fear and selfishness were the root of all problems. He had admirers as well as connections to leadership in the pre– and post–Second World War period and with the beginnings of the European Union. While he seems to have had a significant number of younger university-aged followers, he had a number of detractors as well.

As has been well noted, the Bishop of Durham at the time, Hensley Henson, wrote at length of "the unscrupulous and even unwarrantable use made of well-known names, at the grotesque exaggeration of the advertisements, at the unseemly luxury and extravagance of the travelling teams, at the artificiality of the 'sharing,' at the mystery of the finance, at the oracular despotism of 'Frank.' . . . I refrain from dwelling on the darkest shadow on the movement – I mean the trail of moral and intellectual wrecks which its progress leaves behind" (quoted in "Buchman," Alchetron).

There was also criticism of how the "total honesty" that was encouraged at the Oxford Group meetings (some were over a thousand people) and house parties significantly concentrated on sexual issues, such as masturbation.

In a well-known response to these criticisms, Buchman said, "We do . . . unhesitatingly meet sex problems in the same proportion as they are met and spoken of in that authoritative record, the New Testament . . . No one can read the New Testament without facing it, but never at the expense of what they consider more flagrant sins, such as dishonesty and selfishness" (Garth Lean, *Frank Buchman: A Life*, 139).

However, more unusual was Buchman's public appeasement approach to Hitler. In an interview with the *New York World-Telegram*, published on August 25, 1936, Buchman said, "I thank heaven for a man like Adolf Hitler, who built a front line of defense against the anti-Christ of Communism." This seems an even crazier statement in that, according to a 2024 article on Alchetron, Buchman previously attended the 1935 Nuremberg rally.

In the U.S., the once very famous religious writer Reinhold Niebuhr famously wrote a chapter called "Hitler and Buchman" in his book *Christianity and Power Politics*. (It is very similar to an article he previously authored in *Christianity Century* magazine in the autumn of 1936.):

> Now we can see how unbelievably naïve this movement is in its efforts to save the world. If it would content itself with preaching repentance to drunkards and adulterers one might be willing to respect it as a religious revival method which knows how to confront the sinner with God. But when it runs to Geneva, the seat of the League of Nations, or to Prince Starhemberg or Hitler, or to any seat of power, always with the idea that it is on the verge of saving the world by bringing the people who control the world under God-control, it is difficult to restrain the contempt which one feels for this dangerous childishness. (160–61)

A prominent German theologian who was later murdered by the Nazis, Dietrich Bonhoeffer also pointed out the extreme naïveté of Buchman in his attempts at converting Hitler: "The

Oxford Group Movement has been naïve enough to try to convert Hitler – a ridiculous failure to understand what is going on – it is *we* who are to be converted, not Hitler . . ." (Eberhard Bethge, *Dietrich Bonhoeffer*, 282).

But while the Evangelical Sisterhood would have known about Buchman, there were also the other brainwashing and control techniques of the day. Basilea claimed to have been questioned by the Gestapo twice during the war, though given the substantial influence of her father, who later became Rector of the Technical University of Darmstadt, it is doubtful it was much of a heavy interrogation. Former members of the ESM in Germany have expressed many thoughts about the influence of Basilea's father and his alleged political views at the time. Basilea's "interrogation" would have been shaped by its time, and that would likely have included some influence of Buchmanism (as it was sometimes called). Basilea also often spoke admiringly of the very stark and harsh Prussian military schools and their abusive rituals that were influential in training future leaders of Germany in the years before and after World War I.

Still, given the popularity of Buchman's movement it is likely that the original light-sessions included a much more extreme variation or influence from Buchman's Moral Re-Armament "house parties."

The following is a translated passage of Riitta Lemmetyinen writing in German in an academic paper and later in *Wenn Mauern fallen* from the 1990s, about Basilea and other influences from the Second World War:

> Mother Basilea does not shy away from using an historical example that she herself has experienced. She uses the example of Adolf Hitler and his SS troops to illustrate the relationship of an elite soldier in a spiritual army to their leader. Mother Basilea tells the Sisters that this illustration

shows how a member of an elite troop should be fascinated by their leader and willing to sacrifice everything for him. The SS and their "Führer" belong together because ultimately they are committed to the same cause. The greatest joy and reward of an elite soldier is the recognition and praise of their leader. They seek nothing else.

The Sisters will only be able to be faithful [to] the end if they are willing to be unconditionally obedient. Hitler's regime gives Mother Basilea a model for this. His orders were carried out immediately. Unconditional obedience does not question a command or suggest an alternative. Disobedience always responds with questions: Why am I doing it like that? Am I really capable of that? No, I don't want to do that! What is my opinion about it? By contrast, unconditional obedience says: without hesitation I will do it, because it is the order given to me. I don't need to think about whether it makes sense to me. (171)

Community of Jesus buildings, 1970s–1980. Courtesy anonymous.

This excerpt is absolutely chilling and shows the distorted mindscape of Andersen and Sorensen's teachers who helped them set up their own cult on Cape Cod in Massachusetts. Yet the Community of Jesus founders were in some ways even more extreme. They did what the Germans never did: they performed light-sessions on children. It is a wonder that they were not arrested for what they prescribed, allowed and condoned to be done to children in Massachusetts and at Grenville Christian College. After them, self-styled Mother Betty Pugsley, who succeeded Andersen and Sorensen after their deaths and ran the Community of Jesus from the 1990s until a couple of years ago (though some members who have recently left say she is still de facto in charge), continued in the same pattern of control. This tradition of authoritarian control is that of a micro-totalitarian society.

According to Peter Andersen, his mother, Cay, said, "We're going to do this 'community thing' better. We can do better than these people."

The Founding of Grenville Christian College

Grenville Christian College was originally started in 1969 when the dignified old Catholic building of St. Mary's College in Brockville, Ontario, built in 1918, was leased and later purchased by Al and Mary Haig, along with Charles and Betty Farnsworth, to create a Berean Christian boarding school.

The two families had met when Charles Farnsworth was an associate minister of the Berean Fellowship International. In 1981 Farnsworth wrote an article called "What the Ministry Means to Me," about his life story and becoming the headmaster of Grenville and a follower of the Community of Jesus. It was included in that year's winter edition of the Community of Jesus magazine *Life Together*. In the article he says he first met Al and Mary Haig when they were passing through Dallas, on their way to visit Oral Roberts University. It was around 1966, Farnsworth recalled: "When we met Al and Mary Haig in Dallas, something clicked inside, somehow I knew that we would be working with them someday in the body of Christ."

Charles Farnsworth praying. Grenville Christian College, 1986–87.

The Bereans, based in Texas, were a sect on the far edge of conservative American Christianity at that time. A group called the Bereans had originally been founded as a sect of Calvinism in the eighteenth century in the UK. The philosophy of the earlier sect was that they were trying to be like the Christians in Acts 17:11: "These [Bereans] were more noble than those in Thessalonica in that they received the word with all readiness of mind and searched the scriptures daily whether these things were so."

The Texas Bereans seem to have roots in a U.S. variation of this literal biblical approach from the 1850s. They were on the fringes of the Charismatic Renewal of the 1960s and had much more in common with fundamentalist Pentecostalism than any mainline churches of their day. The Texas Bereans tended to share the revival's most backward-looking views. However, their far-reaching Berean Fellowship sent out missionaries and encouraged the formation of literal faith schools abroad.

The Haigs had heard that the former Catholic Redemptorist seminary buildings called St. Mary's College (built in 1918) on the St. Lawrence River near Brockville, Ontario, had been put up for sale just after the school had shuttered its doors the previous year. The couple was unsuccessfully running a girls' school called Stoney Brook out of a basement in New York while Al was, at the same time, reported to be holding the title of associate pastor to the now widely discredited Norman Vincent Peale at the Marble Collegiate Church in New York City.

Farnsworth (according to his writings) worked with Al Haig for a year at the Stony Brook school, which became a Berean school sometime around 1967 or '68. Farnsworth wrote that "we had a year of exciting ministry out on Long Island; many kids were baptised, and filled with the Holy Spirit, though that faith was not as well grounded as we thought. After a little over a year Al and Mary felt called back home to Canada to establish a school there." Charles Farnsworth also moved to Canada but was called back to

Dallas to continue involvement with Berean International Schools. This involved a considerable amount of "traveling, speaking and preaching" (according to Farnsworth's 1981 personal account in the Community's self-published magazine *Life Together*).

They purchased the seminary building, according to their own accounts, after allegedly cashing in their life insurance policies to secure the down payment in 1969. They regularly repeated the story of first walking on and deciding to buy the property on the same day as the moon landing, July 21, 1969. That fall, they started their own Berean boarding school, with J. Alastair Haig as an independent director of the Berean Fellowship of Canada and headmaster of the school.

Around 1971 or 1972, Charles Farnsworth and his wife, Betty, rejoined the school, with Charles becoming second-in-command. It was reported that, in January 1972, a large part of the Berean Fellowship International disbanded due to financial reasons and scandal. The displaced Bereans and Berean missionaries from abroad were allegedly left stranded. Many came to the new school in Canada. They joined the people who had followed the Haigs from Stony Brook and other random Bereans at the school. The *Waco Tribune-Herald* reported on September 16, 1973, that "the Berean group wrecked itself by internal strife in 1972." There had been a lawsuit and scandal. Property was sold to pay some of the Bereans' debts. The same article also reports, "The Rev. Peter Tovey, president of both World Renewal and the remains of Berean, said in court, 'We felt it was better for our image to change our name.'" It was also reported in Dallas news that the charismatic George Snure of Brockville, Ontario, was on a preaching bill in Texas with Al Haig in 1973. The Snure family temporarily joined the school as part of its leadership around this time.

The remnants of the Bereans were now living on the campus in Brockville. The story put forward by leadership and recorded in Al Haig's book *Headmaster* is that they soon fell to petty squabbling and backbiting with no real vision, leadership or funds to carry the mission forward. Farnsworth wrote of this time that "in fact it got so desperate that Al and I would lie on our faces and pray, 'Lord what needs to happen to bring this work to a fruitful state?'" He added, "We invited many charismatic teachers and preachers to visit, and they would come and prophesy and pray over us, but no one seemed able to give us the direction that we needed" (according to Farnsworth's 1980s personal account in the Community's self-published magazine *Life Together*).

By 1973, the school was beset by structural and financial problems, with a staff deeply divided along divergent theological lines, so the Haigs contacted Cay Andersen and Judy Sorensen to give some "much-needed" advice and direction. These were the same women who had proven their holiness by praying for and (reportedly) temporarily healing their family dog of distemper a number of years earlier. The Haigs had formed a friendship with Andersen and Sorensen after meeting them at a prayer session around 1961 in Toronto. The meeting was transformative for Al and Mary, and they kept in contact with the women for the next decade, inviting them to return several times to lead prayer, healing and teaching retreats to a core group of very conservative, evangelical-leaning Christian families in the Toronto area. Farnsworth had also met Andersen and Sorensen in Cape Cod in the 1960s. The two women had then invited him to be their guest on a retreat to the Sisters of Mary in Darmstadt, Germany, in 1969, where he had been deeply impressed by the work of the Evangelical Sisterhood.

Now, under the titles of "Mother" Cay Andersen and "Mother" Judy Sorensen, they came to speak to the staff about the Community's way of life and its extreme religious beliefs. They had originally planned to stay a few days but ended up staying much longer, teaching daily about how to use light-sessions and how to deploy their version of tough love on students.

Farnsworth had a strong reaction to the visit, writing, "I remember reluctantly going to the motor home where Cay and Judy were counseling and talking to them. I don't know how the subject arose, but suddenly they were talking to me about my father who had died some twenty-five years previously, and all at once I was bawling like a baby, and those two precious ladies ministered to me and comforted me" (*Life Together*, 1981).

As the Mothers' visit stretched longer than expected, the Community of Jesus's distorted theology was preached around the clock: death to self, death to pride, jealousy, disobedience, self-centredness, self-satisfaction and willfulness – "All these are enemies of God," Andersen said, "and stop His life from flowing on this campus" (Farnsworth, *Life Together*, 1981). The Mothers insisted that the school needed a structure, which Anglicanism provided, and that Anglican liturgy should be introduced straight away into the school chapel. It wasn't long before the school was renamed Grenville Christian College after the township in which it was located.

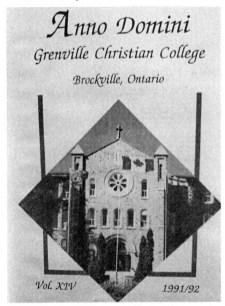

Grenville Christian College flying the official Anglican Church flag beside the provincial and Canadian flags.

According to Al Haig's autobiography, *Headmaster*, which he published with a Community of Jesus–associated press, the staff prepared to go on regular retreats to the Community of Jesus and became members along with the school leaders. Haig wrote about one of his early interactions at the school – a kind of preface to a public light-session by the Mothers – in his book. Here is his account of one of their speeches:

> Sorensen spoke first. "God has given us a scripture first to describe what He is about to do here. The axe is laid to the root of the trees. This college is like a twisted tree that must be hewn to its very roots, in order that a tall, straight fruit-bearing tree can grow in its place.
>
> "Your methods, your way of doing things, your philosophy of education, your ways of dealing with young people, your opinions, your plans have failed. It's time to start all over again – this time, God's way."

Al Haig and Charles Farnsworth were fast-tracked to become Anglican clergy. They were installed as Anglican priests in a ceremony with the Community of Jesus's leading pastor, Arthur Lane, who had previous Episcopal links, taking part in the ceremony at St. James Anglican Church in Kingston, Ontario, in 1976. Andersen and Sorensen were in attendance.

Andersen and Sorensen taught the Grenville college staff how they organized the structure of their lives, which they called "living in community." This involved ministering to each other by "speaking the truth in love," a form of spiritual correction and admonishment meant to bring a soul from the darkness of sin to the light of repentance. It appears that only the three Grenville pastors and their wives initially went to the Community of Jesus for immersion. There, they were subjected to all the community disciplines. In the end, they vowed to accept Andersen and Sorensen as their spiritual directors. Subsequently, no major decision regarding the Community at Grenville would be made without their consultation.

Farnsworth wrote in his article "What the Ministry Means to Me" that quickly the fate of the school changed: "Al and I were going out and praying over those vehicles that they would make it the five hundred miles to Cape Cod" and "within eighteen months we had paid off an impossible one hundred and fifty thousand dollars of debt. Our name was restored in the community and our enrollment began growing larger every year."

However, former members claimed staff were being paid as little as thirty dollars a month. It was part of the new sacrifice of being members of the Community of Jesus. The low-pay situation was addressed at the trial. During the Grenville trial in 2019, Don Farnsworth testified that the college was giving the Community of Jesus about a hundred thousand dollars a year. In addition, many of the teachers were not qualified.

The dignified old stone structures of St. Mary's College, with its vines growing up the front of the building, gave the school the appearance of an ivy league college. Its arched stone entrance and Catholic Redemptorist motto – *Copiosa apud eum redemptio* – which was placed in the mosaic in the front main entrance, impressed parents and gave the group that ran it an air of older established respectability. That motto was later adopted into the Grenville persona and put in its crest. I remember Al Haig asking the Latin teacher to translate it for the gathering of students one day in the gym as we stood near the centre of the crest in the middle of the basketball court. The Latin teacher, put on the spot, had difficulty translating the phrase and stuttered through it. The administration and the staff all came off as uneducated. Even as a little kid I thought, "I don't know anything and neither do they."

Eventually, the story goes, two groups of fifty staff members travelled by bus to Cape Cod to be "live-ins" at the Community of Jesus, where they submitted to the authority of the resident community household to which they were assigned. Thus, the Grenville staff adopted some of the Community's harshest teachings by learning "The Way of the Cross" and how to "speak the truth in love" at the Community of Jesus. Very soon, the Community of Jesus's theology began its insidious and deliberate reach beyond the vowed members of the Grenville Community and into the student population at Grenville, along with the light-sessions.

Community of Jesus compound, 1970s–1980s. Courtesy anonymous.

People weeding a garden at the Community of Jesus, 1980s–1990s. Courtesy anonymous.

Staff members claim to have paid (or tithed) 10 percent of their salaries to the Community. The school also gave a substantial amount of money to the Community, apparently to pay for retreats, as well as to purchase a house in the Community's compound in

Rock Harbor, Orleans, Massachusetts. One former senior member and witness told me in a formal, on-the-record interview, "I am now ashamed to admit it, but I was brought into the room [at the Community of Jesus] as muscle to get Al Haig to submit to the Mothers' bidding on an issue at Grenville."

Everyone on staff at Grenville knew of incidents of physical, sexualized and sexual abuse on students, but because everyone among staff was bonded together in the abusive mind control light-session rituals, they protected each other in a way normal people are not conditioned to.

That this went on for over two decades is almost unbelievable.

The Community's attorney said in a statement via email to the *Cape Cod Times* in response to the trial: "The most important facts speak for themselves: the plaintiffs in a Canadian court case alleged 13 years ago that as many as 45 years ago, individuals at an institution not in any way, shape, or form run or directed by the Community of Jesus, in another location in another country that is hundreds of miles away from Cape Cod, engaged in wrongful conduct against them."

There was no claim filed against the Community of Jesus. There was no finding by the Court that the Community of Jesus had engaged in wrongdoing. What there was was the Canadian plaintiffs' claim that certain individuals in Canada took what they regarded as the "idea" of certain individuals who forty-five years ago had been involved with the Community, and that those purported "ideas" were in some fashion partially "responsible" for the misconduct of staff at the Canadian school.

And yet, "Mother Betty," then leader of the Community, wrote a letter dated in 2000 to the staff at the school, stating that "the vows [to the Community of Jesus] taken by many at Grenville" – including swearing obedience to the group's leaders – still applied. Relationships with other children were discouraged, and almost impossible given the harshness and betrayal of the light-sessions and networks of tattletales that were rewarded for ratting out their friends.

In a retreat tape from the early 1980s titled *Idolatry, Anger, and Lust*, the "Mothers," accompanied by the famous evangelist Peter Marshall Jr., used Luke 14 – "If anyone comes to me and does not hate his own father and mother" – to justify their understanding of idolatry:

> SORENSON: Because I chose God over my children, they were ultimately able to choose God over themselves. . . . I didn't understand it because I thought it was cruel, unloving, and neglectful, but I obeyed God anyway, whether I understood or not. . . . When I was preferring them, when I was spoiling them, when I was turning my back on their sin . . .
>
> ANDERSEN: They were a mess!
>
> MARSHALL JR.: Yeah.
>
> SORENSEN: Because you control them through your idolatry, and they want your idolatry – they want your love, your money, your acceptance, your forgiveness, your leniency – but they hate you for not demanding of them what God wants you to demand of them. . . . You are building up a kingdom of hate and rejection and loneliness for yourself when you do to your children what's by nature our desire to do with them.
>
> MARSHALL JR.: We see this problem over and over in counseling. . . . It's the other parent who coddled them, who tried to make it up to them.

This exchange between the leaders demonstrates the Community of Jesus and Grenville's attitude toward parent-child and student-teacher relationships. This attitude was vigorously enforced at the college. It was also how adults dealt with each other at both the

Community of Jesus and Grenville. Joan Childs, a member of the Community of Jesus and second-in-command at Grenville, confirmed this by saying, "If the people in charge told us to do something, we did it."

Grenville Christian College in 2019. Courtesy Ewan Whyte.

The Art of Deception
The Arts, Music and Poetry of the Community of Jesus and Grenville Christian College

Despite their grounds in human creativity and freedom, it has long been known that music, art and poetry are central to the construction of forms of social order and control. Plato banished them from his ideal Republic. In the case of the controversial Community of Jesus cult, its arts programs are/were crucial pillars in the construction and maintenance of what former members' accounts reveal to be a totalitarian micro-community.

The art, music, architecture, stained glass, popular theatre and writing programs of the controversial Community of Jesus sect are considered by many former members to be self-legitimizing fronts for this charismatic Christian group whose top leadership live lives of luxury while many of its lower-level members live very modestly or abstemiously. Many give much, and in some accounts state almost all, of their money to the group, or work without pay, while taking vows of loyalty and obedience for life. My experience as a young child at the Community from age eight through much of my teenage years, including my forced attendance for several years at its close affiliate, Grenville Christian College, was one of extreme isolation, violence and loneliness.

The sect presents itself as an arts-oriented Benedictine community – despite not being Benedictine. Its leader, "Mother" Betty, was actually its amateur choirmaster for several years, under the name Elizabeth Patterson. It is their amateur choir, the Gloriæ Dei Cantores, that sometimes impresses audiences and often legitimizes them to the unsuspecting outside world. The Community also engages with the wider world through its Christian publishing arm, Paraclete Press; its extravagant basilica with over-the-top mosaics and paintings; and its popular theatre productions, allowing them to present an image of wholesomeness and/or spiritual holiness, depending on the occasion and audience.

Interestingly, but perhaps not surprisingly, it is the leaders who seem to interact most with outsiders and not middle- and lower-ranking members who still appear to remain mostly distant from the public that the organization seeks to impress.

But their creative process, according to some former members, is not all love and donuts. Some recount an extreme and for some harshly punitive creative approach. As one former Sister says, there is

> a great discrepancy coming from the Community of Jesus. This discrepancy is seen clearly in their fantastic claims regarding their artwork, namely their mosaics, their self-proclaimed world-class choir, their pottery and painting and the beautiful delivery of meals to guests, which are a work of art in their presentation . . .
>
> May I say there is a vast discrepancy between what they call beauty and prestige and the lives of the ones that produce this so-called beauty. Has anyone ever interviewed one of the choir members? Does anyone really know the lock and key they live under, or the disciplines imposed for the slightest infraction? Since I worked in one of the areas of art there for a good 25 years, I think I should have a voice. The phrase that explains the discrepancy very well is "they make you a peasant in your own goldmine." By peasant I mean that you do what is told and required of you to do. Your own life is under continuous scrutiny. One lives under the threat of exposure for what they call infraction, therefore one lives in fear continually. They call it obedience and actually it is a vow that one takes which is totally

unbiblical. They claim love is obedience. What they mean is "do what I say or get punished"

Evangelical Sisterhood of Mary, Germany, 2019. Courtesy Ewan Whyte.

Evangelical Sisterhood of Mary banners, 2019. Courtesy Ewan Whyte.

I remember as a child and teenager all kinds of punishments, disciplines and severe corporal punishments. I even remember violence being threatened on adults. Almost always for what seemed trivial reasons, individuals would be put on silence punishments – some of these would extend for months. Shunning and a kind of hyper-gaslighting aspect of light-sessions were just as normalized as it was at Grenville.

As a child I also took part in a Community of Jesus choir and sang in front of large audiences. The obsessive urge of those in authority to impress others, especially outsiders, was oppressive and unforgiving to the children and those of the lower ranks. The Choirmaster was harsh and unforgiving, especially considering some of us were as young as eight. The young boys were there to sing the soprano parts but we were also part of his other obsession. He was covertly sexually preying upon us. Grenville's choir, which later I was briefly forced into, was run similarly.

The Community started their arts program from the beginning of their interactions with the Evangelical Sisterhood of Mary. When I went as a visitor for two several-day visits to the ESM in Germany researching the history of the group, it was beyond shocking for me. There was almost nothing that the Community and Grenville appear to have come up with themselves. The stained glass ideas of the Community of Jesus came from the ESM in Germany, even the fonts the Community used came from their banners.

Grenville also mimicked the Community of Jesus with its choir and its Gilbert and Sullivan student productions. Charles Farnsworth even fancied himself (once a year) a judge of student public poetry recitals, which favoured the most saccharine rhymester-style verse.

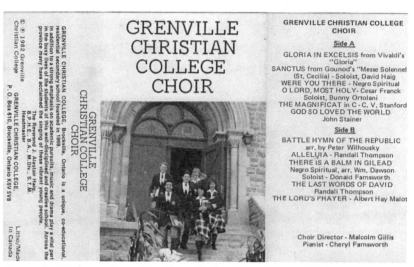

Cover of a 1982 recording of the Grenville Christian College Choir.

This is a cover of one of the Grenville choir's recordings, featuring Don Farnsworth, Headmaster Charles Farnsworth's own son, who would later go on to defend the school in the class action. The son of the other headmaster, Al Haig, is also listed as a soloist on the recording, though both were adults and no longer students at the school at the time.

A good place to start discussing the art and writing of the Community of Jesus may be in an article called "Choose Life" written by Hal Helms, a senior member in the Community of Jesus around 1988 when Elizabeth Patterson was moving to take over leadership of the Community of Jesus. (The Community seems to have become even more arts-focused after Mother Betty took control around 1990.) Helm's piece was published by the Community of Jesus in 1998's *Life Together* magazine.

> Jesus warned that there is a broad road leading to death, and it is a crowded way. He said the way to life is narrow and the gate is straight. Robert Frost said it like this:
> I shall be telling this with a sigh
> Somewhere ages and ages hence,
> Two roads diverged in a wood, and I –
> Took the one less traveled by,
> And that has made all the difference.

Helms ends the piece here, quoting the famous Frost poem out of context, showing he clearly did not understand the poem or its deliberate ambiguities and humour. Frost wrote "The Road Not Taken" in 1915, during the First World War, as a "joke with meaning" for his friend, the British poet Edward Thomas. The two regularly went on walks together to discuss their writing. This poem makes statements, then doubles back, just like the walks of Frost and Thomas. The deliberate opening, as has been commented many times, is like the beginning of a fairy tale, one that could be from Andrew Lang or the Brothers Grimm. The playfulness of fable is misunderstood here as is connotation for denotation. The playful lines of the poem state that the paths were worn really about the same and this is not a choice of a road to death and life. It is, among other things, an internal meditation on indecision and our sense of relating to it in terms of our unconscious or as in fairy tales/parables.

The previous lines in the same poem help to fill out a deeper and conflicting meaning, and as Robert Frost used to joke, "a moment of wisdom":

> Then took the other, as just as fair,
> And having perhaps the better claim,
> Because it was grassy and wanted wear;
> Though as for that the passing there
> Had worn them really about the same,
>
> And both that morning equally lay
> In leaves no step had trodden black.

This twisting of the meaning of things to fit their whims is typical of my experience of the leadership in the Community of Jesus to this very day.

But art is a useful window dressing. As I witnessed, and as former members attested, the way the Community saw and presented itself was as an elite group of individuals chosen by God before the foundation of the world to be part of a select, unmatchable group. The idea that they were producing artistically elevated work supported the claim.

One former Sister shared her experience in creating the artwork for the leaders of the Community to give to Pope John Paul II when they met him in a planned and staged meeting in St. Peter's Square in 1988. That they got such a meeting, given the controversy surrounding their group, is shocking. Surely senior members of the Catholic Church who organized this meeting must have known something was off about them.

> Once I was asked to help design a piece of stained glass to present to the Pope. Yes, our clergy were going to Rome for an audience with Pope John Paul II, the Ecumenical one. Another Sister and I designed the piece. The Brothers did the woodwork. I will speak for myself. I was "put on silence" before this task was given. Can I ask you how one communicates rationally with another human being when one cannot speak? I do not remember if I could write notes. Many times, they informed me that they did not want to hear what I had to say. So, I was not allowed to write notes. I do not remember which was the case. Nor do I remember what the infraction was that initiated the discipline. I only remember the torture of not being able to communicate. I also remember that Thanksgiving Day came during this time. I went to the meal in the Dining Room where all the Sisters were assembled, I ate my meal in silence and then left. [I continued] to work on the stained-glass piece. We had to explain to the ministers who would transport it to Rome via airplane then taxi. They had to be instructed how to put this triptych together, because it was transported in three separate panels . . . The beauty that was exhibited in that elaborate piece of artwork with the Pope's motto carved into the wood and metal neumes of Gregorian chant running through the panels, certainly hid the pain and anguish of the soul of the one who did much of its creation. I'm sure the Pope never guessed.

A visitor in the early 2010s described the Church of the Transfiguration of the Community this way: "No expense was spared in the chapel – elaborate baptismal font, huge carved bronze doors with gold inlaid brass around them, fountain outside the door, organ pipes inside shuttered boxes the full length of both sides of the nave." They also noted a "large mosaic of Jesus at front of the church that I find a little strange and frightening. A looming, almost demonic face of Jesus hovering overhead (maybe I'm projecting here;

Community of Jesus empty basilica, 2019. Courtesy Ewan Whyte.

I was told it was based on Christ Pantocrator, which you can see from the darker right side), arms open with lines coming down to the floor that almost look like leashes, while obedient sheep process up to the top and out the door of light – those doors are duplicated below [not shown in this photo] with opaque glass – the theme is obviously the 'light' of Christ."

But the Community must have a good publicist, since its choir, Gloriæ Dei Cantores, has been written up several times in the *Boston Globe* between the 1990s and 2000s. This despite the investigative news series *Chronicle*, who did a two-part investigative news program on them called "Community of Cult?" in the 1990s; and other Boston media, such as *Boston Magazine*, publishing exposés on the cult. The *Boston Globe* has rarely written anything but puff pieces about their music and art. The soft-toothed piece on U.S. airman Aaron Bushnell, who grew up in the Community and later left on bad terms before he burned himself alive in front of the Israeli Embassy in Washington, DC, on February 25, 2024, was a rare exception.

In one feature-length article from 1999 on Betty's conducting of the choir her husband had created, she goes by the name Elizabeth Patterson, which is particularly telling. The article relates their visit to Cambridge for a year in 1979, where Rick worked with Cambridge scholar and Catholic nun Mary Berry (a.k.a. Mother Thomas More) on plain chant. Later Berry spent lengthy periods of time in the Community working with Rick and others with the choir. She reportedly continued her involvement even after 2000. She died in 2008. She also visited the Abbey of Saint-Pierre de Solesmes, which also has a connection to the Community of Jesus.

A Facebook post from a member of another choir that places her at the Community of Jesus around 1993:

> In about 1993 I, and a friend from my choral group, Ecclesia Consort, picked Sister Mary up at Community of Jesus and drove her to Providence Rhode Island's Blessed sacrament Church where she gave Ecclesia a brief two-hour lecture on Gregorian Chant personally. It was one of life's most amazing things. We then drove her to Boston's Logan and I asked her her favorite chant, which she proceeded to sing gently in a very crowded terminal. She began the Alma Redemptoris Mater with head bowed. She began despite the cacophony around her. When she got about half through, the room was completely silent . . . no lie. It was a transforming moment for me and one I hold dear forever. She was first a loving nun and woman of faith, and second a dedicated and passionate instructor of the Chant. (quoted in Jeffrey Tucker, "Merry Berry and Alma Redemptoris Mater," Chant Café, December 15, 2010)

I remember Mary Berry very well from my time in the choir, as she would give me personal voice lessons. From my witnessing her interactions with members and the choir, she also appeared to be aware of the much darker sides of the Community of Jesus. Berry personally recommended that I be removed from the choir during the time the choirmaster was sexually assaulting boys.

In the *Boston Globe* article, we learn of Betty's relative lack of training in comparison to her husband's Columbia PhD – an undergraduate degree from Millikin University in keyboard and organ, and teaching experience in high schools and night schools. Betty explains why Rick Pugsley Sr., who had started in 1972 when the couple joined, handed it over to her in the late 1990s: "My husband is no longer directly involved in the choir because he's branched into chant. He left me with the whole nine yards of the choir, but this was a joint decision. There is still a lot of breaking information about chant and it is helpful to have an expert consultant!"

Naturally there was no mention that Pugsley Sr. had been exiled from the Community of Jesus to Cambridge, England, for sexually abusing boys a few years earlier; just that he's an ongoing source of assistance on chant. As a child, I witnessed Richard Pugsley Sr. sexually assaulting boys inside the Community of Jesus compound during my forced time there, which another man who was also sexually assaulted as a child by Richard Pugsley Sr. at the Community of Jesus confirmed. I wrote about these assaults in an earlier essay in *Shifting Paradigms* published in 2021, and have testified to them in the bankruptcy case of *Kanaga v. Landon*, on June 2, 2023, in Tulsa, Oklahoma. For me, it was clear that he was there for the boys and not for the music. Andrew J. Hale-Byrne also writes of Pugsley's sexual abuse of children in his time as choirmaster at the Community of Jesus in his 2016 book, *Grenville*. Former senior members of the Community of Jesus claim there were several families paid off to be silent and former member David Manuel addressed it in his 2008 affidavit, which has been made widely available through the Rock Harbor Truth website. Here is a passage that starts at line 119:

Another person in that circle who was not practicing celibacy was Rick Pugsley, who was director of music at that time.

It came to Barbara's and my attention that sometime in the 1990's he had used his position to make sexual advances towards some of the young men to whom he was giving voice lessons.

In typical cult fashion, the Community of Jesus keeps its dirty secrets secret.

We would never have known about it, except that we were named as codefendants in a sexual harassment lawsuit . . .

Unbeknownst to me, my wife and I were apparently on the Community of Jesus's board of directors at the time of the incidents, and so were named along with the others.

To the Community's and our great relief, the case was settled out of court for $187,000.

At the time, Barbara told me that Rick had been involved in a similar case, with [name redacted] . . .

That case was also settled out of court for a payment [of] $30,000 a year for ten years.

Rick is over in Cambridge, England, now on a stipend, "doing research" and not coming home. ("Affidavit of David B. Manuel, Jr."[1])

A favourite at the Community of Jesus were more popular parts of Bach Cantatas; "Jesu, Joy of Man's Desiring" was a constant. I remember singing it in their choir on many occasions. Later I would hear the famous piano version by Dinu Lipatti from 1946. The level of emotional depth and musicianship is just on another level altogether from the amateur versions of the Community. That said, Bach played modestly or badly is still Bach.

---

[1] https://www.rockharbortruth.com/_files/ugd/4659bf_a9634ca9282246e585616c2fec3d669c.pdf.

An audience member shared their experience of attending a concert of the choir in the 2010s:

The concert itself: one of the elderly Brothers stood up front the whole time, to prevent anyone from coming forward I guess, though with a smile on his face; the singers came on from the side very quietly, the men in tuxes and the women in long gold dresses – the older ones with fancy red Chinese jackets over the dresses; they started with Bach's motet "Komm, Jesu, Komm" – the opening text translates "Come, Jesus, my body is weary – I am becoming ever weaker . . ." – they sang with a light, soft, bright, breathy sound and equivalent smiles on their faces – precise and in tune but without any expression or inflection resembling the music's relation to the text. I thought to myself, how are they going to sing Vaughan Williams's "Dona Nobis Pacem" [a big piece with orchestra] with a sound like that? I found out soon in some early Mozart selections that they do *forte* too, when asked. A very firm, ringing sound. They all take voice lessons and theory lessons from the conductor . . . or his assistant . . .

The women sang the Poulenc "Litanies to the Black Virgin" flawlessly in terms of tuning and blend, but with little inflection. The conductor was very business-like – everything clear and in its place – but almost deliberately without any visible emotion, mouthing the words, or facial expression of any kind, even in the big moments of the Vaughan Williams. Finally at the beginning of the last big passage his face warmed and the faces of all the singers responded instantly. Up until then, they had been as expressionless (but precise) as his conducting, very still, fairly natural looking, but with little animation, movement, or apparent effort of any kind . . . The whole performance had a weird feel to it – it felt as though a performance hadn't really "happened" – there was no drama, no spontaneity, no engagement – but the audience was appropriately awed . . .

The strangest thing happened at the end of the concert: The conductor extended the silence at the end, as is typical, but in this case rather static. The audience then began to applaud, and soon stood up slowly for the obligatory standing ovation after such a work. But then when the conductor and soloists left the stage, the clapping just quickly petered out before even one curtain call. Even with such a spectacular piece having been just been performed with a high level of accuracy, there was no energy in the room – no sense that what should have been a riveting performance of a penetrating piece of music had just happened . . . the energy just left the room suddenly, and everyone just sort of looked at each other as if to say, "well that was excellent, wasn't it – I guess it's time to go."

Before the performance the observer had introduced himself to "an older, well-dressed couple" that was sitting next to them. They were Episcopalian and would occasionally attend Community of Jesus services to hear the choir. He continues:

> They were very friendly, and it turned out they were "oblate" members, beginning about 10 years ago. They are members of a Episcopal church and come to CofJ . . . now and then, mainly to hear the choir. They said they had no requirements as "oblate" members other than to come when they could and "contribute." I asked plenty of leading questions to see what their awareness of the cult-like aspects of the community were, like, "do the families each have their own house?" "Do the kids go to school outside the community or to college?" (answer: some do,

some don't) – but they seemed to be well-off members of the community without a clue about the darker aspects of the past.

Mother Betty, it turns out, is a "poet" as well as a musician. Her poem included in the Community of Jesus self-published magazine *Life Together* in the autumn of 1988 includes an anthology section of poems in honour of Mother Cay. An excerpt of Betty's poem reads:

Now with inner eyes we strain to catch faint celestial colors:
Perfect . . .
Pure . . .
Hinting of solid essence.
Now with inner ears we strain to hear unheard sounds . . .
Singing not marked by soul or strife, but selfless praise
and adoration.

This is the kind of writing we would expect from an aspiring young teenage poet. This is not written by a child, but by an adult close to fifty years old at the time, with public pretensions to "high" art and soon to be the leader of this highly authoritarian sect.

The tired line "not marked by soul or strife" is not the kind of poetic effort we expect from someone who portrays themselves as a major artist. To the reader, it comes off as a beginner's work, grasping for poetic thoughts or phrases, reaching for something profound but instead falling beneath the quality of a Hallmark card. Expecting any innocent passerby to read it and take it as "high art" is delusional at best.

Perhaps it is the performing of the music of Bach and Palestrina that may make someone think they are also a creator of art on the same level?

Here are a few poem excerpts of Community of Jesus poets

(from their self-published *Life Together* magazine in the memorial edition for Cay in 1988) in all their literary glory.

I want to be very different
I want to be very different,
from who I am today,
It really, impressed me,
all because of Mother Cay.
– A Brother

In Romsey Abbey
Loft, flowing, fleeting song,
Scripture, chorus, tolling long
Beating color, grace and blessing . . .
– A Brother

Fight the Good Fight
Across the fields the tromping soldiers go,
with naught but bloody bayonets to show
their conquering spirits sought the heavenly tide
to ride, and finding power beneath their hands
– A Brother

These works are not exceptional by any stretch. That the group presents/considers themselves to be exceptional and their arts exceptional is what is telling. The lack of self-awareness is sometimes astonishing.

When the Community hires professional artists to decorate and paint their basilica, it is a slightly different picture. Even so, the painting of African biblical figures on the walls of their basilica as almost white is embarrassing to see. That said, it fits well with the Christian nationalism history of the Community, as David Manuel and Peter Marshall Jr. covertly wrote the Christian nationalist bestselling book

The Light and the Glory in the Community of Jesus compound.

Their music program is good for an amateur choir but not on the level of a truly professional choir, as the *Boston Globe* music specialist explained in 1999. It does impress those unfamiliar with professional performances. In my view, a quick listen to the British choral group The Tallis Scholars' performances enables you to hear the gulf between a truly professional singing group and the Community of Jesus choir.

The following poem seems to describe experiencing a light-session, which members know so well. The psychological intensity of them over time can bring people to doubt themselves on the deepest emotional levels. It is a very effective control technique.

Upon your return
I thought while you were gone upon the things
you'd said. Those words still clear, so pure, with wings
and flames descended to my heart and burned.
– A Brother
(*Life Together*, 1988)

The Community saw and presented itself as an elite group of individuals chosen by God before the foundation of the world, and believed their creative endeavours were born of this divine selection.

A former Sister again:

I need to add one other thought. They use this beauty as their "blood-washing." They point to it and say "Look at the FRUIT." They have no idea what they are saying and what an absolute ludicrous statement this is. First of all, the fruit they are referring to are the nine fruits of the Spirit as put forth in the Bible (Galatians 5:22). These are love, joy, peace, patience [or forbearance], kindness,

GENTLENESS, goodness, [faithfulness,] and self-control. If one is truly filled with the Spirit of the real God, one exhibits these characteristics. They cannot be faked. After living in this place for over twenty-five years, I can say there is NO REAL FRUIT there. Sorry! Their artwork does not whitewash the vileness of many of the hearts there, nor the sinister way they control the people and innocent children who have the misfortune of being brought there or being born there. This is a travesty which needs to stop. Can you imagine being born into this place and then HOME-SCHOOLED on top of it. You would never know there was a real world out there. Your values would be skewed and you would never be able to apprehend the marvelous, wonderful, full, beautiful love of the real God who created you. How sad. All you know is their skewed doctrine of error.

Let's end with these notes from an academic visitor, who wishes to remain anonymous, to the Community of Jesus compound in the 2010s:

I noted that U.S. news reports from the last ten to fifteen years seem to be unaware of any cult-like activity; a former senior member said the children now are not even allowed to go to school [though several members claimed that this was up to the parents and that not all were home-schooled]. When one of the founders children was going to the public school as a child, they had to wear special uniforms and were not allowed to invite other children to the community or participate in any social or extra-curricular activities. Now the isolation seems to be almost total.

[The] guest book in Paraclete House has mostly just names listed for oblate retreats, with only a handful of separate guests and church retreats over the last few years. It was interesting to note that three out of about ten members of the "oblate board" were from Daylesford Abbey. I wonder if they are aware of the mind-control cult nature of the community?

It seems so much of their connection with the outside world is inner-directed toward their music and arts programs mostly at the Community; no mission to the poor or disadvantaged. Paraclete could be seen as a service for spirituality, but it is probably a for-profit business – a lot of money is being spent and raised from somewhere for the benefit of the community itself. They aren't commissioning new music that I'm aware of, or writing new books of spirituality based on anything they're doing, beyond a big coffee-table book about the church and its artwork. The houses are large and pristine from the outside – I saw another young woman sweeping stones at the edge of a driveway with a push broom, which seemed unnecessary, perhaps punitive – but during several walks around the neighbor-

View of the front entrance walkway to the Community of Jesus with part of the basilica visible to the left. Courtesy Ewan Whyte.

hood throughout the afternoon, I saw very little activity of any kind (like kids playing, etc); once I did hear someone practicing their singing.

I went to Lauds, done forty-five minutes before the main Sunday morning service, which is a hybrid Anglican/Catholic mass with chant propers sung by a "schola" of eight Sisters, one of six such groups. For the Lauds, a large number of Brothers and Sisters were present, dressed in special beige cassocks with full-length green vestments (front to back) over them, and wooden crosses. Non-celibate Community members wore these too. A young woman in regular clothes, clearly a community member, seemed depressed and sat next to other Sisters who were vested.

The chanting was antiphonal between the men and the women – a very nice, smooth, light sound, and fairly fluid and comfortable with the antiphons from the *Graduale Triplex*, which they all sing from. But the Psalm verses themselves were very machinelike with no accentuation – explanatory material about the music program at COJ talks about using the Latin because it matches the chant, and the book Sister Alicia lent me to use (her *Triplex*) had English penciled in throughout. But it didn't look like there was time for awareness of the text (though they did observe the mid-verse pause). They are trained to genuflect if they make a mistake.

For the mass, most of the Sisters and Brothers left, which was strange; other Community members came in, including two women with six to seven young girls (around eight to ten years old, I think) who looked quite shell-shocked and sad. I asked a Community member about participation, as was told that was usual – people had other things to do – which I thought was strange in a community where liturgy was apparently so central. This would seem to be the main service of the week – it's not like they live far away – and Mother Betty again was not there. (She "had meetings since very early in the morning." On Sunday?) The organist played the hymns very fast – the community was almost reciting the words while being very light on the tunes because there wasn't enough time to really sing them. The sermon was pedantic and seemed to be from someone who is probably a high-level "enforcer" under Mother Betty. The parable of the sower was the text, but the theme was related more to a quote from Francois de Fenelon [a seventeenth-century French bishop] on the cover of the leaflet, which I found quite saddening when I first sat down:

It is hard to believe that a loving God could allow us to suffer. Does it please him? Couldn't he make us good without making us miserable? Certainly he could. God can do anything. Our hearts are in his hands. But he does not choose to spare us sorrow.

Notes on Attending the Civil Trial Against Grenville Christian College

Many former students came from both the United States and across Canada to attend the 2019 trial against Grenville Christian College. Some former students came from as far afield as the United Kingdom. It was eerie to be together in a room resembling a classroom so many years later. This time, the room was a courtroom.

I knew it was going to be filled with unpleasant moments and I suspected I would be shocked by the lies that the defenders of the school would present, but it was so outrageous at points that it seemed like watching performances of poorly trained actors interspersed with moments of professional lying. The school's lawyers' arguments seemed outrageous to me at times, talking about Grenville's abusive and sexually assaulting former headmaster Charles Farnsworth (as featured on the CBC's *The Fifth Estate*) as if he was a caring but strict parent.

It seemed unbelievable that the school was finally being forced to account for itself in court. Its affiliate by shame, the Community of Jesus, was referred to throughout the trial, often synonymously with Grenville, but was not officially part of the lawsuit. The former students' lawyers were confident of their position. They seemed to know that they had a winning case. They were, however, facing a formidable and larger defence team of lawyers assembled for the school. It was a very expensive legal team.

The school's defence lawyers appeared to be leaning far more toward old-school intimidation tactics, hoping to scare away the former student victims/witnesses. One of the lawyers had even written a book that was interpreted by some of the former students as detailing how to behave in court to confuse/upset/intimidate a witness to achieve a desired outcome.

We, the former students, some still very traumatized all these years later, would meet in court every weekday between September 16 and October 17, 2019, to watch the lawyers fight the case out. It was hard to watch former students' distress from witnessing the former staff and former student prefects lie in court in defence of the school and the influence of the Community of Jesus.

Day after day this went on. Although the trial was scheduled to last for five weeks, several witnesses for the school apparently declined to appear, causing some embarrassment. At one point there was discussion in the courtroom by the lawyers about when a witness for the school was going to appear. He never did.

It was emotionally gruelling. There were times when the former students attending would meet at a restaurant during the lunch break, just up the street from the court, and recount past traumas to each other, many still in disbelief that anyone in their right mind would think that doing such things to children was a good idea. One day after leaving the court for the day, a former older student I had known at Grenville followed me out onto the street and, through tears, told me and Dr. Ruth Marshall, a University of Toronto professor with whom I've been working to research the school, about being repeatedly sexually assaulted by a former adult staff member at Grenville. He spoke about the staff member frequently pursuing him and bringing him into his office constantly alone and asked if I remembered him being singled out. I had to think for a little bit then I was overcome with a moment of dread – yes, I remembered. I had forgotten the creepy circumstances around his frequently being taken out of class by the adult staff member. Just like so many others who have experienced traumatic episodes, our minds find ways to consciously forget. Unconsciously I am not so sure that is ever possible. The process of remembering is a strange one of blocks of memory being blotted out. Bringing them back into focus is sometimes more painful than its idea.

One student, a former staff kid I knew well, who had flown in from the U.S. Midwest to attend the trial, still has trouble remembering almost anything from her whole childhood and teenage years at Grenville. Her friends have to tell her what happened to her and how she responded to things and sometimes even who she knew. She later lived at the Community of Jesus before leaving.

She has a rare autoimmune condition that is almost only found in those who had significant childhood trauma. This and similar conditions seem far more common in former (especially long-term) Grenville students and those who had childhoods in the Community of Jesus. There are many people in this kind of situation.

Perhaps the most stressful days in court were the days when Headmaster Charles Farnsworth's son and long-time staff member Don Farnsworth testified in court. He was defending the school, his father and the association with the Community of Jesus. Membership in the Community of Jesus was a fraught part of the arguments as well. There was a conscious (as far as former students were concerned) attempt to distance Grenville from the Community of Jesus. The following is an exchange from court transcripts about his membership and vows to the Community of Jesus, led by lawyer Loretta Merritt.

> LORETTA MERRITT: Q. This is the Community of Jesus vow of service.[2] If you could, sir turn to page 9. I'm sure someone told us earlier in this trial, but I've forgotten, sir. Can you tell me the difference between the first vow and the final vow? Is that all done at the same time, or is there some time gap in between, or do you remember?

---

2 *Community of Jesus Vow Service,* https://www.rockharbortruth.com/_files/ugd/4659bf_4678dec3aba846808a55d69df87fd41e.pdf.

[DONALD FARNSWORTH:] A. Usually there was a first vow in that you – you made a vow or a commitment to – to try to follow the ways of – of the community. In this case – in this occasion, it was the Community of Jesus, yes. The second vow was just a little more perfect – permanent vow, sort of like an engagement is to a marriage.

Q. I see. Got it.

A. So, no they wouldn't be taken at the same time. You would have experienced that life and decided if you wanted to go a step further.

Q. Okay. Got it. So, sticking now if we could to the Community of Jesus member's first vows, and this is on page 9, in – in almost the middle of the page, there's some bolded words there that'll help you find it. It says:

> I express my obedience to you, Jesus, through my yieldingness and submission to the Community of Jesus and to my spiritual Mothers, Mother Cay and Mother Judy.

That's the vow you took, sir?

A. That's the vow I took back in the seventies.

Q. All right. And then if we can, turn over to page 16, and this is the final vows, it says at the top of the page. Sorry, go right over to 17, what I'm going to quote is actually on 17. I just wanted you to see that it was the final vows there on page 16. Turning over to page 17, again the part that's bolded, it says:

> As part of this vow, I promise, with the grace and help of God, to let the Holy Spirit, with the help of my spiritual Mothers and brothers and sisters, correct, admonish, chastise, and discipline me

according to the disciplines which are deemed most beneficial for the sanctification of my soul.

And you took that vow as well, did you not, sir?

A. Yes and I just want you to – to – to be clear that we were – we had accepted their authority as spiritual leaders. This was a – a – a vow for their resident community members. We were one group that was not residents of the actual Community of Jesus, so at that time, this was the best fit. They changed this after a while, because we were not residents, even though we called ourselves residents in the field. So, we used their vows, because that's the – those are the ones for their own community.

Q. Right. I understand that and – and – and your spiritual authority at Grenville would have been Father Farnsworth, your father, and Father Haig; correct?

A. At the time of these vows . . .

Q. Yes.

A. . . . . it would have been Father Haig, yes.

Q. It would have been Father Haig and then later Father Farnsworth as well?

A. Yes.

Q. All right. And what was the worst, most humiliating or harshest discipline ever imposed on a member of the Community of Jesus, to your recollection?

A. Imposed? I'll have to think about that. To a faculty or a community member, one of us?

Q. Yeah.

A. Well, there were times when it was strongly recommended that we – we spend some time at the Community of Jesus, for spiritual growth. I wouldn't call that a harsh discipline. There might have been a time when – when we as a member of our staff would have been asked to – to be on some type of discipline. Now, that wasn't like a students' discipline. That would have been where we were – had more structure in our lives, you know, I think probably the worst thing was when someone had a reduction in pay.

Q. Okay.

A. That's always tough.

Q. You thought that was tough, okay. And if I could, sir just continuing on page 17 there, I think it is, at the bottom of that paragraph that we were just reading, it says:

> I promise, as part of my vow of conversion, to live in the light

Live in the light is in bold there.

> Together with the called members of the Community of Jesus, being both a giver and recipient of the truth, which is intended to put my carnal come of flesh life to death and to build the spiritual life of Jesus Christ within me.

So, I take it the method by which that was implemented, the – the promise to live in the light and be a giver and recipient of truth, the method by which that was implemented was light-sessions; correct?

A. No, it wasn't the only method. That was a method. That was a time when we as staff members, community members, obviously in this case, would get together and we would share things, our own feelings, things that we had that we felt were wrong in our own lives, or if someone in our group we felt needed something to change in their lives, we would bring that up. However, that is not the main reason, or the main method. The main method was if we were to see someone, or in our interactions, if we had interactions with them and they – we thought they were out of line, we would speak to them. We wouldn't let it go. We wouldn't talk behind their back. We would – and that was a – an important rule, never talk about someone else, unless they're right there in front of you.

Q. All right.

A. So, in our daily lives. Our daily lives were meant to be honest.

Q. So, I get – I – I – if I'm right, I – I – I get that the issue you're taking with my question is the method, as opposed to a method, so I'll rephrase it. Is it fair to say that light-sessions were a method by which that promise to live in the light and be a giver and recipient of truth was implemented?

A. I – I agree with that, yes.

Q. All right. And those vows, sir were usually made in Cape Cod?

A. These vows, yes.

And later on, here is another exchange between the lawyer and Farnsworth.

[LORETTA MERRITT:] Q. All right. And would it be fair to say that the Community of Jesus was heavily involved in the direction of Grenville, you got a lot of support from them, as to how you could live, as a community?

[DONALD FARNSWORTH:] A. As a community, yes.

Q. And one of the things you learned from Community of Jesus was correction is not rejection; right?

A. Yes.

Q. And if people did not agree with what the leaders said, or were angry, it would have been frowned upon for them to publicly come out and say this is wrong; correct?

A. Yes, it would have.

Q. It was not an open democracy, was it, sir?

A. That's a good question. I don't think it was an open democracy. I think there was – there was the opportunity to – to disagree, but – but yes I think sometimes those demands were imposed more than suggested.

Q. Okay. You all went along with the suggestions from leadership, because that's what was being part of the community was, and you trusted the leadership; correct?

A. We trusted them – the leadership.

The next witness in the 2019 class action trial against Grenville was the last headmaster of Grenville Christian College: Gordon Mintz. He was accused of significant emotional and physical abuse of children at Grenville. He was later featured in two CBC *Fifth Estate* episodes, where former students described some of the abuses he put them through. He was previously quoted as dismissing any abuse at Grenville in an article in the *Globe and Mail* just after the closing of the school in 2007/8. In a dramatic scene televised on *The Fifth Estate*, CBC journalists waited for Mintz outside his work at CFB Borden and confronted him on camera. This was in 2021 after the trial.

As a child I had witnessed Mintz's abusive behaviour in action at Grenville. It shows how out of touch he was to come to court to defend the school as one of its former headmasters and a man who took vows of loyalty and obedience to the Community of Jesus.

As of the summer of 2025, Gordon Mintz is still an active Anglican priest and is currently serving in some sort of assistant capacity at a Collingwood-area church.

Currently on the All Saints' Anglican Church website: "The Rev. Canon Gordon Mintz is a retired Canadian Forces Chaplain and part of our clergy team at All Saints, Collingwood and

Regional Ministry of South Georgian Bay."

At the time of the trial he was a senior padre in the Canadian military. He wore his formal military uniform to court. It looked and felt like he was showing his power and authority. It was slightly intimidating to watch him enter the court and sit on the stand just because of the persona of the uniform he wore. I had the slight feeling of "not again." *Are they going to pose their way out yet again?*

Here are excerpts from his 2019 testimony.

[GEOFF ADAIR:] Q. Sir, I understand you are an ordained Anglican minister?

[GORDON MINTZ:] A. That is true.

Q. And tell me I started off correctly by calling you Lieutenant Colonel?

A. That is true, but Gordon is just fine too.

Q. Okay. And you're a Lieutenant Colonel in the Canadian Armed Forces I understand?

A. That's correct, as a Military Chaplain.

Q. And you are – you have a Bachelor of Arts degree from the University of Western Ontario in Commercial and Administrative Studies?

A. Correct.

Q. And a Master of Divinity from Wycliffe College, University of Toronto in 1992?

[. . .]

[LORETTA MERRITT:] Q. All right. Sir, you're still an [avowed] member of the Community of Jesus, are you?

A. I actually have no idea. I was an oblate, and I haven't been there in a while, so I really don't know what my status is – it's not an active relationship.

Q. All right. When was it last active?

A. That's a good question. I went there for a personal retreat in 2014 . . .

Q. Okay.

A. . . . when I was in Ottawa.

Q. Okay.

A. I think it was 2014–2105, and I was there for three or four days, and I hadn't been there for years since then, probably 2008, probably since Grenville closed.

[. . .]

Q. But let me understand, did you take the first vows and the final vows of the . . .

A. No.

Q. . . . Community of Jesus, or not?

A. No, I took oblate vows.

Q. Yeah, that's what I mean, but there were first vows and final vows for the oblate members?

A. I never took – I took one set of vows at Grenville.

Q. Okay. And those vows were the Community of Jesus vows, right?

A. Correct.

[And later on . . .]

Q. You were on the board?

A. Yeah, I was on the Board of Directors.

Q. When?

A. That would have been at the time I was serving the parishes in the Diocese of Ontario.

The following is Mintz being presented in court with a letter from a former student's parent on the Grenville "Honour System":

[LORETTA MERRITT:] Q. It's a bit hard to read, but it says, "Your method of obtaining information about what other students are doing or have in their possession, e.g. Walkmans, is not the Christian way." And further down, the start of the next paragraph, "Publicly humiliating students is again appalling." And then, if we go back the previous page, so we're on the third page, "the General Comments," the, the parent's name is "Stock." I am looking at the third point Stock makes, "Don't approve of one student informing on another, no mercy." And then, if we go to page, the ninth page, you sort of have to count your way in. I am going to have a question at the end of this.

[Gordon Mintz:] A. No worries.

Q. Okay. So this is the one, it has sort of a, a count of numbers on the right side in handwriting and on the left, or sorry, on the, on the left side, on the right, it starts with, "The features we most like."

A. Yes.

Ms Merrit: Okay. So go, if we go down to "Criticisms."

> As we understand it, you have a so-called honour or caring system, which is [a polite] name for encouraging children to tell tales. This is simply horrific and has to be stopped. It is one of the worst features of all totalitarian societies that rewards are offered for denouncing non-conformists.

Ms Merrit: Q. So, having looked at all those criticisms of the honour code and tattling and this not being Christian way, and being described as "horrific," looking back now from where you are today, do you think maybe that having the children tattling on each other was maybe not such a good idea?

A. I would say the honour code, if it was applied over exuberantly and children, and students were trying to appease staff by ratting out on their fellow students, I would agree. And the fact that sometimes staff let that happen or encouraged it, I would agree. The fact that the honour code was explained to be something where we as a community and a student body could live in the most healthy way possible, and hold each other to a high standard, I don't agree. So I think it was misapplied at some point is where I am going with that.

Q. Okay. So . . .

A. But I, in general, I support the honour code, and, and we lived by it.

Q. So, so the honour code itself was not necessarily a bad thing, the difficulty arose in its application?

A. Correct.

Gordon Mintz claimed to not remember many things at the school on many occasions during his testimony and cross-examination. It was retraumatizing to hear staff and former student prefects appear to lie deliberately on the stand, defending Grenville and the Community of Jesus. Some students seemed devastated to hear Mintz repeatedly claim to have no memory of the offences done to former students during the sixteen years he was a member of staff at Grenville starting in 1984 and finishing in 1999, with several months' hiatus at the Community of Jesus, where he was a long-time member.

But this was my and so many others' experience of dealings with sworn members of the Community of Jesus at Grenville Christian College.

The extreme gaslighting techniques took away our words to explain to the outside world what had happened, and left us with unfathomable and unseen wounds to outsiders that made us unnecessarily vulnerable. We were often left with severe self-esteem issues and frequently a lack of proper social boundaries. Many students would go on to struggle with these injuries throughout their entire lives.

Throughout the trial there was some changing of the student audience. But it was steadily very well attended. At one point a larger courtroom was used due to the former student turnout. People would attend for a few days, then they would disappear. Some found it too difficult to attend for more than a few days, while others lasted only a few minutes some days. Only a handful went the whole distance. I took time off and attended most days. A few days I felt sick as it was overwhelming to watch some of the defenders of the school lie, but I couldn't turn away; I had to see what would happen. I remember well the final arguments. I had a feeling that it was a one-sided trial, that Grenville seemed to have, despite their expensive defence, a very poor case. But I still had lingering doubts as the school had somehow managed to deceive so many for so long as I had witnessed in the past. Maybe they would even do it again, my doubting self thought, but surely not. Overall it was a grim experience. I can see why some people sometimes just don't want go through the gruelling court process.

Justice Janet Leiper issued her decision on February 23, 2020, finding in favour of the plaintiffs. As part of her decision she wrote, "Grenville knowingly created an abusive, authoritarian and rigid culture which exploited and controlled developing adolescents who were placed in its care. In doing so, it caused harm to some students and exposed others to the risk of harm. This meant that the headmasters profited from their positions, reputations, status and control over a cowed student body."

She concluded that "the evidence of maltreatment and the varieties of abuse perpetrated on students' bodies and minds in the name of the COJ [Community of Jesus] values of submission and obedience was class-wide and decades-wide. The plaintiffs have established that this conduct departed from the standards of the day. The school created a place to mold students using the precepts and norms of the COJ. It obscured its more extreme practices from its patrons and parents. It failed to keep records of the more extreme discipline practices."

Grenville "knowingly created an abusive, authoritarian and

rigid culture which exploited and controlled developing adolescents who were placed in its care." It was, as Margaret Granger, one of the representative plaintiffs, put it to me, "a precedent-setting case, and the first historical abuse case to win at trial in Canada."

A Discussion Between Ewan Whyte and Suzan Ewton About Her Experience at the Community of Jesus

This is a discussion with Suzan Ewton, one of the first nuns at the Community of Jesus. She was still a teenager when she first came for a vacation from the Netherlands to the early Community near Orleans, Massachusetts, in 1969. She saw much of the early madness at the Community and was a witness to a significant amount of abuse. At the time she first arrived, she was nineteen and still learning English.

Ewan Whyte: How did you get in there?

Suzan Ewton: I was in the Netherlands, and there were several reasons why I wanted to leave the Netherlands. One was I was uncomfortable with my life the way I was living it because I knew I was going down the slippery path. And in 1969, that's when the drugs came in and I was afraid. I was working at an airport and my boss, and his wife, they were like my parents that I never had. Of course I had parents, but I mean, I looked up to them as totally trustworthy. But my boss was not. He came after me sexually and I was devastated. I didn't tell anybody, but I wanted out. So I got away. And my sister Ellen, she was Corrie ten Boom's travel companion and secretary, she is the one that led me to Christ when I was twelve years old, I always wanted to be like her. I wanted what she had. And I don't know why, but there was just a desire in my heart. At fifteen, I had started to feel that something had to happen.

I was so mad at God that I didn't get my way. I showed him that I wanted to do the right thing and I forgot the details, but I rebelled and I said, I will never pray again. I never read that Bible again until I was nineteen. I went to Austria with a little group of young people for skiing, you know, just a ski vacation for a week. And I was like, those mountains – the beauty just spoke to me. I said, my God, there must be a God because this could not just happen. So I called my sister Ellen after that and I said, Ell, I want to leave Holland and I don't want to be an au pair somewhere in England or France. I want to go to America. She says, "Well, let me think." That was about two years before the Community was formed. That's when Cay and Judy had help in their homes, you know.

WHYTE: Yes.

EWTON: I met a couple of people and they had a guest house on Cape Cod. And, you know, girls came there for the summer and helped clean and make beds. They said maybe you can go there for about six months or so or three months or however long you want to go. Unbeknownst to my sister, it had turned into a community, a cult. She just thought it was a family and I would just stay in the guest house and help out and, you know, have fun and go to the beach and whatever. She did warn me. She said, "Now they have a beach there, but you better not bring your bikini. It's better to be in a bathing suit over there." And I thought, what the hell do you mean? I wear what I want to wear. I never wore a bikini. So that's how I got into the Community of Jesus. Within three months I was brainwashed. I came in October 1969 and by January, I mean, I was [scared] into becoming a Sister. Of course my English was terrible. I mean, that's crazy but I, you know, I feared I would end up dead or I would have children that were sick or I would end up like my dad who took his life. [Scared] into [the notion] that if I would not be obedient to God, as there was as a call on my life to be a Sister, a celibate Sister, I would get cancer, get all the horrible things that could happen when you're out of God's will.

WHYTE: Wow.

EWTON: Those are the actual words that were spoken to me. So then I was so devout and I was treated so well by that time. Heidi [Laser], who had been top notch with Cay and Judy, she was on her way down, being put on discipline, and I took Heidi's place. That made me, of course, feel better and secure. And then there was another girl that I was working with ironing and cleaning and doing. Her name was S. and she later married. She left. She wanted to run away but was caught and brought into the kitchen of Zion. And Judy walked up to her and slapped her in the face so hard. And, you know, it's like whatever she did, you do not want to do, because you don't want to be on that side of those two people. It was just such a play on innocent minds, what not to do and what to do to stay in good graces. And that's how you lived.

WHYTE: How awful.

EWTON: That's how it creeps in. It's little by little, by little, and by the time you can breathe, you are under water. And you can't breathe anymore. And you'd do anything to survive.

WHYTE: You were just learning English and still a teenager –

EWTON: I didn't even know what those people were. There were those girls and they had all a gold ring on their finger. And then that S., the girl that ran, that left, said, "Oh, they're Sisters." Well, I was, you know, from the Netherlands, Dutch-reformed non-Catholic. And I said, "Sisters? They don't look alike. Why did they wear the gold ring just because they're sisters?" You know, nothing occurred to me. Nothing made sense. She said, "No, they're *Sisters*, like nuns." I said, "Like what?" "They're all like nuns." And I almost threw up. I mean, Catholic nuns. Are you kidding? I was not even allowed to play with my neighbours if they were Catholic. And here I was.

WHYTE: That's so deceptive.

EWTON: I literally got ill. I wanted to go home right there and then, you know. I was in one of the rooms, put up in one of the rooms to get well. And then I was told the reason I was ill is because God was calling me to be a nun, a Sister. That's how the whole nightmare started.

WHYTE: And Cay and Judy told you this?

EWTON: Yes. And Heidi [Laser] was sent to me. But yes, Cay and Judy were the ones that told me that.

WHYTE: And do you remember Mother Basilea and Mother Martyria?

EWTON: I came after that. Judy had just come back from Germany. They were at that point, all against Mother Basilea.

WHYTE: But they used light-sessions right at the very beginning?

EWTON: I think so. It started out with Bible study every morning in the dining room at Bethany. And then I think pretty soon those turned into light-sessions.

WHYTE: You were extra vulnerable in your situation with your father taking his life when you were such a young age. Would Judy have known that?

EWTON: I was looking for security. And it was not that I was not loved in my family. I was the most loved child. I know I was deeply loved by my mom and by my dad and by my sisters and brothers. Lord, I was physically loved. I was held. I was kissed. But I was looking for a better life. A better life because we were as poor as poor can be. And I wanted more in my life than being poor. So you go to America and you then end up in a beautiful setting. You think you just made it?

WHYTE: Rock Harbor Manor was beautiful back then.

EWTON: My gosh, and the *food*, I gained twenty pounds. I never have had such lovely food in my life. Peanut butter and Fluffernutter sandwiches and hot toast in the morning with honey. English-muffin toasts. Goodness sakes.

WHYTE: How old were you when your father passed?

EWTON: I was ten.

WHYTE: Ten, that is so young.

EWTON: It was a very unhappy marriage.

WHYTE: And Judy made you destroy the photos of your father?

EWTON: They made me throw everything that had to do with my home, with Holland, with the Netherlands, with my family, in a box to be thrown in the garbage. I couldn't have anything to do with anything to do with the Netherlands, with my mom, with my family.

WHYTE: Did they let you speak with your family?

EWTON: No. No. I had to write a letter to my mother saying "I will never see you again, I will get in touch with you. Do not get in touch with me. If you do, you will never see me again." I had to be totally cut off from my family.

WHYTE: Did you ever see your mother again?

EWTON: In the very beginning, my mum was allowed to come. But then I was sent to Bermuda for some reason I can't remember and she was allowed to come to Bermuda. Then at one point we had to go in a light-session. Well, my mother said to them, "You know what? I think you two think you're Jesus Christ and you are not." Well, that was the beginning of the end. The next day she was on a plane and gone.

WHYTE: Wow. But she –

EWTON: She spoke up.

WHYTE: Did you ever see her again after that?

EWTON: Yes. After I ran away in 1986. I have had wonderful, wonderful memories with my mum since then. I went back to the Netherlands. I was introduced again to my family because they hadn't seen me for fifteen, fourteen years or so, though Mom saw me. Maybe for two years out of the seventeen years. I can't remember dates and times that well. But I went back to Holland and got reacquainted with my sisters and brothers and my God, I have the best family. I have such a lovely family, and some great times with my mum. She came to our wedding with my sister Lucy and then she came over here [to the U.S.] every year. I went over there every year as well. It was just absolutely nothing but amazing, amazing memories with my mum. And my whole family.

WHYTE: Cay and Judy were trying to deprive you of this.

EWTON: They did deprive me. They didn't try, they *did*. They destroyed me.

WHYTE: What do you think Judy's objective was with this?

EWTON: They wanted me for themselves. It's that simple. They wanted my total devotion. I also think they were afraid that I was going to talk to my sister Ellen, who worked for Corrie ten Boom. And Corrie was a big influence here in the United States in her time, some thirty-odd years ago. She was with the Billy Graham [Evangelistic] Association and everything else. There were several movies made. I couldn't have anything to do with Ellen. She came for a visit at one point when Heidi was on discipline. Well, my sister Ellen knew Heidi from the first time she had come two years before I came, that's when they met. They had a wonderful time and became great friends. They were like sisters. Well, she and Corrie ten Boom came to the Community after I'd been there. Corrie said, "There's something wrong. They're separating children from their families." It's the worst thing you can do. So Ellen happened to go downstairs to the laundry because she did that before on her earlier visits. She just went downstairs. Well, by this time, you didn't make one step outside of where you were told where you could go. And she saw Heidi who was on discipline. Heidi was on silence with her head down and looked horrible. Ellen asked, "What is going on with you, Heidi?" Heidi was just motioning because she couldn't talk. She was not allowed to talk. So that's when Ell went to Cay and Judy, and said what's going on here, and that's why Ellen and Corrie ten Boom never came back.

WHYTE: Well, Corrie ten Boom was a remarkable person. Before her exceptional actions in the war, she was the first woman watchmaker in Holland, an incredible level of skill and accomplishment.

EWTON: I still can see her hands, her beautiful hands.

WHYTE: Then she was caught hiding Jews during the war and sent to the camps. I think her father may have died in the camps shortly after?

EWTON: No, her daddy died in The Hague in the prison before they were shipped to Ravensbrück, along with her sister Betsy.

WHYTE: Did Betsy survive?

EWTON: Betsy died in Ravensbrück.

You could ask, why couldn't they have done something about [the Community of Jesus]? Why didn't the Billy Graham Association do something? But it didn't happen that way.

And it made me stronger. I became a stronger lover of Jesus in that hellhole than anything. You see, once I saw the truth I knew the Community had nothing to do with Christianity. I knew that, so I never lost my love for the Lord, as others did. And I get that. I so get that. But it didn't happen to me. I only became stronger because I had nowhere to turn. I didn't have a family to turn to when I was put on silence or when I was put on my front for twenty-four hours with my forehead touching the ground. I could not move, and for what? I don't know. I was forced to confess all kinds of things, thoughts about Cay and Judy and children and whatever. I wrote grocery bags of confessions. I don't even know what they were. I just pleaded with God to be with me, to help me through this hellhole somehow to get me out. Either strike me with disease, with cancer so I could die or to get me out of there. One of the two. But I can see why people also can go the other way. If that's the love of God, forget it. I don't want it. I've become much more compassionate of others.

I just love people. I love the needy. I can't see a reason to hurt anybody after what I've been through. And I did have to hurt people. I had to yell at Heidi things that I didn't even believe in, because I had to report that I did what I was told to do. You know, it is just such a sick, disgusting, vile place.

WHYTE: I am wondering about your experience with Christian nationalism at the Community of Jesus. And the idea of the Community of Jesus, that before the foundation of the world the Community of Jesus was determined to be, you know, chosen by God. But that seems a variation of the idea that America was chosen to be a Christian nation.

EWTON: Oh I totally disagree with that.

WHYTE: Me too, but Cay and Judy were deeply into this.

EWTON: Christian and nationalism, those two words I don't think go together at all. Just do the nationalism. It's all about what the Community was about, money, white money, position.

In Christianity, *true* Christianity, Jesus came for the lost and the poor and the sick and the lonely and the downtrodden. So those two just don't go together to me at all. But. That's what the Community of Jesus was: very white and very, very money oriented.

WHYTE: Yes. It was like somebody's humanity was higher. It's like they were a better human if they had money.

EWTON: Exactly.

WHYTE: And the children were pretty low ranking.

EWTON: Children were nothing. They were, I think, more of a burden almost. Yes they wanted the children because they needed to keep the Community of Jesus going. But they were not respected.

WHYTE: I remember Peter Marshall and David Manuel's attitude toward children. As a child there it felt like I was viewed as truly a third-class citizen.

EWTON: You experienced that. You lived it.

WHYTE: Do you remember David Manuel when he was writing the book *The Light and the Glory*? I think it's still the most widely read book of Christian nationalism among Evangelicals to this day.

EWTON: Yes.

WHYTE: If you could talk about the circumstances of the writing of that book that the general public doesn't know about?

EWTON: David and Peter Marshall were writing a book. They were doing it together.

WHYTE: Yes.

EWTON: I would have said it was more Peter Marshall; he lived at Zion. He and Edith, his wife, were in bunk beds, I think. They were not allowed to sleep together but in bunk beds. Now, you know, what I remember, is that Peter Marshall had to write two chapters a day down in the cellar of Zion. It was cruel of us, you know? I remember Bill Andersen, Cay's husband, and myself were in charge of seeing to it that he wrote those two chapters every day and had to stay down in the cellar until it was done. I mean, he got food, I'm sure, but just the fact to be forced to write. But you must know how hard that would be.

WHYTE: Oh yes.

EWTON: So that is what I remember of the writing of that book. Peter Marshall had a beautiful church on Cape Cod in Dennis – East Dennis – and then he started to go to those Monday night meetings [at the Community]. Members of his church started to come to the Monday night meetings. Then Peter Marshall had lunch once a week with Cay and Judy. You know how it starts out so sweet and everything is wonderful. He had Cay and Judy's approval. You know, Catherine [Marshall, his mother, who wrote the Christian bestseller *A Man Called Peter* about his father] was even alive then and she and a whole bunch of people came down and they did not see it at all, what was going on even then. Though Catherine never came back. They came on a retreat and they did not see eye to eye with Cay and Judy. But anyhow, it's so deceiving. It starts all warm and fuzzy and it ends up like a cat with claws. So that's what I remember about that. That book was forced. I mean, you know I never read it. But ah, there are even credits, and I'm not proud of that, in the first edition. In the front page, the credits to the people that helped him writing that book – and my name was in there. Later on I thought, O Lord, I'm so sorry I put that man through what he went through. But you did what you were told.

Peter Marshall had been under horrible disciplines in that community. He was not that high ranking by then. He was forced to watch his dad's movie, you know *A Man Called Peter*.

And had to look at all the horrible, dumb idolatrous things his dad did, as a way of cutting down that beautiful movie? And he was separated from his wife. There's no love story there now. Trust me.

He went through hell. But he stuck with it.

WHYTE: Who put him on these disciplines? Was it Judy, Cay and Judy? And what had he done to be on these disciplines?

EWTON: It was a discipline that is put on the person just so they would be under their control. To be pushed around. To be scared. Fear is instilled in a person, and you're so scared to get out of God's praise or God's punishment or whatever. There's no rhyme or reason why. Talking to somebody you were not supposed to talk to or saying the wrong thing, but God forbid you said something against Judy or questioned them. You name it. Just find the crack in a person's life that they can put their heel in and rip it open, and the person is left emotionally bleeding and gasping for air. You'd do anything they tell you to do, just to be at peace. But you never were. And none of us had the gall to stand up against them. That's the one thing I can still get so mad about. I didn't tell them to shove it and to go to hell and get out of there, you know. But you just didn't. You just didn't. The thought occurred to you, but you didn't know where to start.

WHYTE: But you were so young when you got in there.

EWTON: Oh yes, nineteen. My brain wasn't even developed.

WHYTE: You were a teenager.

EWTON: Yes.

WHYTE: The light-sessions. How would you say they affected you? What was your first encounter with a light-session?

EWTON: You would do anything not to be the subject of a

light-session. You sat in a circle with everybody and if you were the one that was on the carpet that day for one reason or another, you have to listen to your best friends throwing you under the bus. You could not defend yourself. You had to sit there and take it, and well, it's horrible and humiliating. Some of the light-sessions I've been in, men and women were totally humiliated to nothing. Of course, mealtimes became light-sessions too. People that you loved, that you were friends with, suddenly turned on you. It broke you in a thousand pieces and you did not know how to gather yourself together again afterward. You just wanted to die.

I was the important one with Cay and Judy and people looked up to me, because I was the link between them and Cay and Judy. The next thing you're in front of two hundred and forty people in their chapel and you're being humiliated and you're slapped in front of all those people. That happened to me and after I was put in the basement on silence for six months at a time not able to talk to anybody, being force-fed, then being starved, being slapped, being kicked, being thrown, and that's not the worst. I was not the only one, but it happened to me and it broke me.

WHYTE: It's remarkable the way you came through it.

EWTON: But still the pain is there. They take a piece that cannot be restored. The idea that scars make you stronger, tougher, I don't believe it. They just make you aware to never, ever put anybody down. To never disregard any human being for who they are, what they believe, or what they are doing. You love them through it and you accept where a person is and you minister to them with food or love or whatever they need to survive their trials in life, or just to live.

WHYTE: Yes.

EWTON: It was also a loss for me to walk out of that community because I lost the people that I was connected to. You know that it's better to lose it, but it's still a loss. And it's also a grieving process. There is life coming out of a cult. I've been away from there since

1986. But still, you're grieving. For me it was the loss of seventeen years of my life, the most formative, wonderful years of somebody's life are gone. That's a big loss.

WHYTE: I still have trouble with this.

EWTON: I can only imagine your pain.

WHYTE: What amazed me about Cay and Judy was the way they would hook people in, but they would hook in people who were vulnerable, people who were either young or if they were older, they didn't have a perspective on the world. It strikes me as almost consciously evil what they did.

EWTON: Not almost. It was one hundred percent, a thousand percent evil. It was totally evil.

WHYTE: Yes, it's totally evil what they did.

EWTON: The saddest thing to me, and the most maddening thing, was they accused and wanted the confessions out of people that were their darkest secrets. Most of the time they were trying to get into quote, unquote, "sexual sins" – lesbian or homosexual or whatever other sexual orientations. Yet after Cay died, Judy Sorensen, who had to go to an insane asylum in a grey jumpsuit after Cay died, told the Sisters –

WHYTE: Yes?

EWTON: Judy said, well, you all know we were lesbians. When Lucy told me that – she had heard it herself – I got so mad. I could have killed! Out of all the accusations they dragged Sisters through, including myself. Because it never occurred to me. So they slept in the same bed. When I was little, I slept in anybody's bed wherever it was warm and wherever there was room. It was not a big deal. I slept with my mum, with my sisters. So Cay and Judy sleeping in the same bed never gave me a second thought. That's not where my mind went, but their mind went there.

You think back then. Judy sometimes would be kind to me when Cay was mad or something, and all hell would break loose.

WHYTE: Cay was jealous.

EWTON: Oh she was the most jealous. And I see that now, later on. I think that's where the hatefulness of Cay came in.

WHYTE: I was wondering about Betty. And because I found Betty to be imitating Judy in savagery.

EWTON: It's though she had evil spirits in her. She was very smart, Betty was. She was one smart woman, you know, Betty Pugsley, intellectually.

WHYTE: She's still reported to be de facto leader of the cult. Though, XX's daughter has officially taken over. It's likely even some of the members don't even know for sure.

EWTON: I think Elizabeth Pugsley is somewhere in Italy. She has removed herself physically from the community now? She probably sees the whole Community mess breaking open. I have a feeling that she does [not] want to be there when it happens.

WHYTE: Yes. And they are reported to have an excessive gun-hoarding situation now. According to accounts, they're training some of them as a militia.

They're doing gun training with even some of the grandpas. This is the word coming back from multiple, multiple witnesses. One person showed me a photo of a cache of the guns.

EWTON: I believe it.

WHYTE: I know that they early on, they took the guns out of the Community of Jesus. There was a gun in Rock Harbor Manor. Peter Andersen, Cay's son, described the situations with the guns, in a formal interview with me in Ireland when I visited him there a couple years ago.

And I had other interviews as well about this. And I think they made a decision early on to not have guns at the Community, because if there were, someone upset from light-sessions, they may pick up a gun and start using it.

EWTON: Yeah.

WHYTE: And somewhere along the line, more recently, accounts claim they've reintroduced guns. Now the vulnerability of the Community is that they covered up sexual assaults on children by adult members.

Richard Pugsley Sr., the choirmaster, sexually assaulted several boys. I would hide from him. I was laughed at when I complained to adult members.

He would put his hands on the boys' private parts. He was a very evil man. A really, really evil man. According to our research he's living in Cambridge, England, at the moment.

Ewton: Wow. Well, he fled the country.

Whyte: And appears to be, or has been, protected by Mother Betty.

Ewton: A sick, sick situation.

Whyte: Yes, but I hope, with this book, it will potentially give cause for authorities to look into them. Because of what is going on with the children. That the children have to grow up in this environment is insane. And that Aaron Bushnell did what he did and said and wrote about the Community should be noticed.

Ewton: I only remember the last name Bushnell, and I cannot put any face to them. Sometimes it's so frustrating.

Whyte: His grandparents [Aaron Bushnell's] would have been your age; they came in through the Berean Fellowship into Grenville Christian College. And that's how they got in. I mean, you remember that everyone at Grenville was a sworn member of the Community of Jesus when I was there.

Ewton: Sure, I remember when it happened.

Whyte: Could you talk to me about that?

Ewton: Judy went up to Grenville. I don't know how they were connected, but they went up to Grenville, and I will never forget what they said. The axe was laid to the roots. That was the Scripture. And Grenville was the tree. And Cay and Judy were the axe and it was laid down to the root to destroy the tree but to leave the root and to rebuild. To rebuild Grenville into obviously the Community of Jesus, part of them, and that's how it started. I remember a lot of those new members from Grenville coming to the Community and all the hair had to be cut and they had to have the dresses be long, you know, the whole nine yards and working hard and gardens and digging, whatever they had to do. It was a huge deal when Grenville came to the Community and it was in the summer. There were all these light-sessions and we had to stay up of course, until the light-sessions were over. It went on forever and ever and ever with the Haigs and the Farnsworths.

WHYTE: I'm hoping something can be done for the children that are still in there. The life outcomes are often very poor for the children.

EWTON: I think they may not even go to a public school anymore.

WHYTE: They're described by recent members as mostly home-schooled at the Community of Jesus now, as Aaron Bushnell's friends claim he was.

EWTON: You know, my brother-in-law, Bob Stamps. He went to the diocese, the Episcopal Diocese of Massachusetts. He asked them, what on earth is going on in that place and why can't you do something about it? They are Episcopalians but they were not under the diocese. Somehow all that bishop could say is there's nothing we can do. There's nothing we can do. And Bob says that is such a crock . . . Of course you can do something about it. They never did.

WHYTE: What was his full name and what year was this?

EWTON: Bob Stamps. Robert Stamps. He's married to my sister Ellen. He was the chaplain at Oral Roberts University for seventeen years in Tulsa. Then he went to England and he was dean of a school of theology there for I don't know how long. Then they came back here to Tulsa. That's how I ended up in Tulsa, because they had a home here.

WHYTE: You have sincerity. Tolstoy talked about this, and I've always found this to be incredibly accurate. Tolstoy's observation that somebody may have literary craft or knowledge and style, but utter sincerity overrides everything and is more powerful than anything else in writing or communication. I think this is very true.

I travelled to the Evangelical Sisterhood of Mary.

EWTON: You did?

WHYTE: Yes. As a researcher, and I travelled with a U of T [University of Toronto] professor, and I have to say, visiting the Sisterhood was shocking. This was in 2019. What I found about the Evangelical Sisterhood of Mary stunned me was how Cay and Judy copied almost everything off the Sisters of Mary.

EWTON: Really?

WHYTE: They did nothing original with their cult that I could see. They just copied almost everything. And of course, Cay and Judy had the German leaders over to help them set up their own sect in the United States, to teach them how to perform light-sessions on people and all the rest. Cay and Judy took the light-sessions to an extreme. Light-sessions all the time because light-sessions were at a set time in Darmstadt in the Sisters of Mary, but Cay and Judy changed that and their light-sessions in Massachusetts could happen at any moment. They took a sect that was already very controversial and then it's like they put the sect on steroids and made it that much worse when they recreated it in America.

But when I was there and looking at the grounds and the font of the banners I couldn't believe how they copied everything. It was an extraordinary moment. It was like a healing moment to see, okay, this is how they did it.

EWTON: Was it not that the Community of Jesus was supposed to be an extension of the Evangelical Sisterhood in Darmstadt and then they changed their course and made it their own?

WHYTE: Yes, that's what multiple accounts repeatedly claim to have happened. I actually saw a light-session by accident in Darmstadt. It happened when I was quietly reading in a chair not visible from the desk where the nun was overseeing the little bookshop. This bookshop is very similar to the Community of Jesus setup, because everything was originally copied at the C of J, including the printing house.

I was waiting there because I believe Professor Marshall had to take a call. I was waiting for what seemed a long period of time, quietly reading over some of the material and things of the Sisterhood that were for sale. I think the Sister who was at the desk forgot that I was there because it was a substantial amount of time. Then a younger Sister came out to speak with her and the much older Sister screamed at the younger Sister and the harshness from the woman who was the Sister who was in charge of the bookstore was so over the top I thought this is exactly like Cay and Judy. She turned and saw me afterward, and she was embarrassed because she had forgotten that I was there. The nun who was showing us around and talking to us later on apologized for this. And I was thinking to myself this is light-session all the way down.

To me, it was incredible to witness that and to really see the ESM in comparison to the Community of Jesus, the way they have their arts programs, the way they did their calligraphy. It's just shocking. The Community now has a holiday mansion in Barga, Italy, in the mountains north of Florence. It is advertised as Mount Tabor Ecumenical Centre, a kind of arts centre but when we spoke with workers there who were members they disputed whether it was an arts centre. There was a previous art exhibition months earlier that was still on the walls, though there were no more visitors.

EWTON: Who lives there?

WHYTE: Well, it looks like it's for Betty. And, you know, the rich of the Community of Jesus leadership to go to and just have a holiday mansion that masquerades as an "arts centre." They call it an arts centre. And they entertain members of the Catholic Church in Italy there. They seem to have members of the Catholic Church in Italy over to have meetings and some sort of exchanges. There are photos of dignitaries from the Catholic Church at the mansion all over their website. They're completely buying it because of an

American monsignor named Timothy Verdon. He performs masses in the cathedral of Florence. I spoke with him and told him about the sexual assaults of children and about this abuse at Grenville Christian College. And it's amazing the way he, you could see he appeared to know that it may be true. But he did not want to turn on his friends from the Community of Jesus.

EWTON: Wow.

WHYTE: It is just astounding the way – the way that guy carried on. He appears to be their most powerful enabler. I would like to warn the Catholic Church in Italy, for what some of their leadership has done in getting involved with this sect.

EWTON: Well, why don't you?

WHYTE: I tried when I was there but it proved to be a difficult thing to do. All those kids, any of those kids – they could be me. It *was* me. I wanted someone to do something for me as a little kid in there, but no one ever did. I know how much it would have meant at the time. I'm an atheist, but that would have been the Christian thing to do.

Aaron Bushnell, Trauma and How the Body Keeps the Score

On February 25, 2024, Aaron Bushnell filmed himself on his phone, walking in his official U.S. Air Force combat uniform toward the Israeli Embassy in Washington, DC. He was live-streaming on the Twitch platform. In it he films his face, then the video drops slightly to where we see he is carrying a large metal water bottle in his left hand. He is calm, and his voice seems resolute as he starts speaking. He says, "I am an active-duty member of the United States Air Force. And I will no longer be complicit in genocide."

He briefly pauses, then adds, "I am about to engage in an extreme act of protest, but compared to what people have been experiencing in Palestine at the hands of their colonizers, it is not extreme at all."

He continues: "This is what our ruling class has decided will be normal."

He keeps walking toward the front gate of the embassy. He stops, placing his phone in front of him so his actions will be clearly visible in the video. He turns and walks the few steps, stopping near the front gates of the Israeli Embassy, then turns to face away from the gate toward the camera. He pours a clear liquid from the bottle over his head, puts his Air Force cap on his head. He says, "Free Palestine." A voice sounding at a distance is heard saying, "Hi, sir, can I help you?" There is a pause of a few seconds as Bushnell has trouble lighting his clothes on fire. The voice, closer now, says again, "Can I help you?" Bushnell finally lights the fluid on the ground and he bursts into flame. Bushnell shouts "Free Palestine" five times in anguish through tall flames engulfing his body. He collapses, motionless, apparently unconscious, before someone turns off the livestream recording.

I knew Aaron Bushnell's family both from when I lived in the Community of Jesus compound in Massachusetts and from when I was a young student at Grenville for three years before he was born. His grandparents were members of staff at Grenville and were devoted to the Community of Jesus. Both his parents were involved with Grenville Christian College and later moved to the Community of Jesus, where Aaron grew up.

His grandparents on his father's side, according to former staff members, were Americans stationed in Africa in some sort of capacity with the Berean Fellowship International that was based in Dallas, Texas. When this group disbanded around 1973 they were apparently stranded by the collapse of their organization and they joined the sole-surviving Berean School in Brockville, Ontario. Shortly afterward they adapted to the new changes as the Berean school transitioned into Grenville Christian College. They accepted a new lifestyle that incorporated the beliefs and disciplines of the Community of Jesus, which was expected with the shifting membership requirements of the college, as was testified to in an Ontario court in 2019. Bushnell's father was older than me and grew up at Grenville, where I knew him, and he made frequent visits to the Community of Jesus. Former members have stated that

Aaron Bushnell with his cat, Sugar. Courtesy anonymous.

Bushnell's mother also was a member of staff at Grenville at the same time and came from the Community of Jesus.

Aaron Bushnell, according to those very close to him that I have spoken with, was born into the Community of Jesus and was mostly home-schooled there with only a brief time in the public school system during high school.

I found his act very upsetting because I saw a young man of twenty-five who, like so many young people I have known from the Community of Jesus and Grenville, was behaving in a way I recognized. Former children of this group have, in my opinion, a kind of similar, some might even call it collective, trauma from the light-sessions and other severe discipline practices they experienced starting from a very young age. These have been well documented in the New England *Chronicle* news program in the 1990s, CTV *W5* news program in 2016, and the CBC *Fifth Estate* TV news program in 2021 followed by another TV news program in 2022. I have written about some of them in my feature essay in *Toronto Life* magazine (in 2021) as well as in my long article in *The Globe and Mail* (December 2023) and elsewhere.

According to his friends (both more recent and older) that I have spoken with, Aaron Bushnell described the intense and abusive mind-control meetings once called light-sessions. These were discussed in multiple very public mainstream news articles and in news programs in the weeks and months following his self-immolation. His act has not left the public consciousness and will likely be present for some time.

Most major news outlets around the world reported on his actions at the time. A street in the Palestinian city of Jericho was even named after him.

The *New York Times* wrote an article titled "U.S. Airman's Winding Path Ended in Self-Immolation to Protest Israel." *New York Magazine* and *Tablet* magazine wrote feature articles on Bushnell and his self-immolation, and both consulted me for my extensive research on the group as did other news outlets like the *Boston Globe*. His act divided the public around the world. There were even supportive protests as far as Taiwan and Japan.

There are also more recent articles noting the one-year anniversary of his self-immolation for and around February 25, 2025, including one from *The Nation*.

It is my view that Aaron Bushnell was deeply affected by his childhood and home-schooling in the compound of the Community of Jesus. As I was quoted in *Tablet*, in March 2024, "It makes sense that Bushnell developed such an extreme zeal for social justice. When you are mistreated as continuously as we were as children, you develop a strong desire to protect the helpless. But you also struggle with the hypocrisy and evil you were raised with. You see people who call themselves the chosen people of Christ regularly beating and abusing children, destroying them physically, emotionally and psychologically. You develop a passion for rooting out bullies and hypocrites. But because your every gesture and thought is criticized and controlled, you don't have any real critical thinking tools."

I spoke with many who were close to Bushnell, and from these discussions, it seemed that he was a very kind and sensitive person who deeply identified with those children suffering in the genocide in Gaza. The hardness that it took for him to do what he did is in no small part a result of the inner strength he gained from willfully not being entirely emotionally crushed by his childhood. I consider myself in no position to judge him. That said, I think he was very unstable.

Aaron stated in a Facebook post a few months before his self-immolation:

> I am an anarchist, which means I believe in the abolition of all hierarchical power structures, especially capitalism and the state . . . I view the work we do as fighting back in the class war, which the capitalist class wages on the rest

of humanity. This also informs the way in which I want to organize, as I believe that any hierarchical power structure is bound to reproduce class dynamics and oppression. Thus, I want to engage in egalitarian forms of organizing that produce horizontal power structures based on mutual aid and solidarity, which are capable of liberating humans.

In the same document, Aaron explained why he was committed to doing mutual aid work in solidarity with the unhoused:

I've always been bothered by the reality of homelessness, even back when I was growing up in a conservative community. I have come to believe in the importance of solidarity politics and I view the enforcement of homelessness as a major front in the class war which must be challenged for all our sakes. I view helping my houseless neighbors as a moral obligation, a matter of social justice, and a matter of good politics. If I don't stand with those more marginalized than me today then who will be left to stand with me tomorrow.

I view enforced homelessness as a societal failing and a crime against humanity. I believe that no one deserves to be deprived of basic human necessities. I believe that homelessness as an involuntary condition must be abolished.

The works of Bessel van der Kolk and Gabor Maté are, from my perspective, invaluable to understanding Aaron Bushnell but also the children and former children of this group and beyond.

In Dr. Bessel van der Kolk's famous book, *The Body Keeps the Score*, he quotes another MD, Dr. Martin Teicher, on the effects of extended childhood trauma: "Research on the effects of early maltreatment tells a different story: that the early maltreatment has enduring effects on the brain development. Our brains are sculpted by our early experiences. Maltreatment is a chisel that shapes a brain to contend with strife but at the costs of deep enduring wounds. Childhood abuse isn't something you 'get over.'"

It has been my observation that so many of those who in childhood have had extended amounts of time in the Community of Jesus and Grenville Christian College seem to have significant difficulties in adjusting to the outside world if they leave. The number of suicides is absolutely shocking. For some, even reaching an average level of social skills is very challenging.

It really does seem that those with extended childhoods in the Community of Jesus and Grenville Christian College often leave with brain imbalances that appear to be permanent.

Dr. Bessel van der Kolk writes about traumatized children in his book, describing the impact of feeling a lack of security and stability, of feeling chronically unsafe and of feeling unsafe in one's body. This situation, when sustained, leaves individuals tuning out their inner voices, so to speak. The result can feel like being almost outside the self.

The ignoring of your inner voice or gut feeling is an ongoing struggle for so many I have interviewed. Those who were traumatized as children at Grenville and the C of J when they were very young seem to have trouble registering danger in its many forms because they were conditioned by experience to override and ignore these obvious signs. It was present and they somehow normalized it. It was just such a common pattern.

Van der Kolk, Gabor Maté and others write about trauma being in the past but how its imprint can also extend to the present and can affect our capacities long into adulthood on many levels, including how clearly we think – or fail to do so.

Gabor Maté writes in his book *In the Realm of Hungry Ghosts*,

> The greatest damage done by neglect, trauma or emotional loss is not the immediate pain they inflict but the long-term

distortions they induce in the way a developing child will continue to interpret the world and her situation in it. All too often these ill-conditioned implicit beliefs become self-fulfilling prophecies in our lives. We create meanings from our unconscious interpretation of early events, and then we forge our present experiences from the meaning we've created. Unwittingly, we write the story of our future from narratives based on the past.

. . . Mindful awareness can bring into consciousness those hidden, past-based perspectives so that they no longer frame our worldview. "Choice begins the moment you disidentify from the mind and its conditioned patterns, the moment you become present," writes Eckhart Tolle. "Until you reach that point, you are unconscious." . . . In present awareness we are liberated from the past. (350)

Yet Van der Kolk cautions: "Long after a traumatic experience is over, it may be reactivated at the slightest hint of danger and mobilize disturbed brain circuits and secrete massive amounts of stress hormones. This precipitates unpleasant emotions, intense physical sensations, and impulsive and aggressive actions. These post-traumatic reactions feel incomprehensible and overwhelming. Feeling out of control, survivors of trauma often begin to fear that they are damaged to the core and beyond redemption."

In hearing about the details of Aaron Bushnell's story from his close friends I see these patterns all there. I also found this to be very difficult to manage.

Van der Kolk writes further: "After trauma the world is experienced with a different nervous system. The survivor's energy now becomes focused on suppressing inner chaos, at the expense of spontaneous involvement in their lives. These attempts to maintain control over unbearable physiological reactions can result in a whole range of physical symptoms, including fibromyalgia, chronic fatigue, and other autoimmune diseases. This explains why it is critical for trauma treatment to engage the entire organism, body, mind, and brain."

It is unfortunate that many of the former children (of non-leadership) from the Community of Jesus and Grenville Christian College tend to be on the extreme end of this. The high suicide rate is a flag to the immense suffering underneath.

The lack of family or weak family connections and poor support networks significantly impacts the recovery and life outcomes of those who were deeply hurt. I found in Gabor Maté's and Van der Kolk's writing about the lack of support situations around survivors to be depressing as it struck me as incredibly accurate. It also, for me, pointed to those who manage to recover to some extent while not undermining the significance of how incredibly difficult it is for those who, through no fault of their own, are alone in their struggles.

It was an unexpected coincidence that while researching the Community of Jesus at its source sect the Evangelical Sisterhood of Mary in Darmstadt, Germany, I came across a mention of a world-famous person who had a relation there. One Sister was very proud of this person, who was spoken about anonymously and at length to me, but not one of the Sisters would say who this person was. It was a bit of a shock when ex-members of the Evangelical Sisterhood later told me after I left Germany who the famous person was. Dr. Bessel van der Kolk was a visitor in his twenties to the Sisterhood in the late 1960s with his family where he was the personal translator for Peter Andersen, Cay Andersen's son, for several days. His family connection to the Evangelical Sisterhood, according to former members, went much deeper, as ex-members adamantly claim his father was a senior lawyer for a large oil company and that he was a financial patron of the ESM. One of Bessel van der Kolk's siblings even joined the ESM.

A former member said that it is very questionable whether he would have even known about the more extreme levels of what went on there. One former member thought it would have been hidden from him. His wit and sense of humour about Mother Basilea was laughingly remembered by some.

Ex-members also shared with me that his father had enough pull to get the young Bessel seated beside Billy Graham at a speaking/meeting in the Netherlands during the late '60s, and then they recounted stories of the young Bessel's humour again.

Peter Andersen wrote Bessel van der Kolk asking him to speak with me about the ESM and childhood trauma. I have a copy of this missive. It didn't happen: famous people are inundated with requests. I also tried reaching out to him directly for comment about childhood trauma when I was writing a long article on Grenville for the *Globe and Mail*. I understand that if someone googled me and read my writing on my childhood and teen years of growing up without parents in an extreme Christian Nationalist cult, which accidentally went viral a couple years ago, I would look like a person with too much to live down. The publication of my long essay "The Cult That Raised Me" in *Toronto Life* magazine came at a considerable emotional price – though the sheer amount of feedback from the public was considerable and reassuring at the time . . . and then there is silence.

I think about Aaron Bushnell often.
From Aaron's will:

> I am sorry to my brother and my friends for leaving you like this. Of course, if I was truly sorry, I wouldn't be doing it. But the machine demands blood. None of this is fair.
>
> I wish for my remains to be cremated. I do not wish for my ashes to be scattered or my remains to be buried as my body does not belong anywhere in this world. If a

time comes when Palestinians regain control of their land, and if the people native to the land would be open to the possibility, I would love for my ashes to be scattered in a free Palestine.

Episodes in Cult Chasing

A few years ago, I set out with my research partner, Dr. Ruth Marshall, a professor of politics and religion at the University of Toronto, to get a clear and current perspective on this sect as it is currently, and those closely associated with its past and its present enablers.

Ewan Whyte at the Community of Jesus.

Months and months of obsessive, painstaking research have turned into years that have taken us to Cape Cod several times, as well as Germany, Italy and farther. I have talked with dozens of ex-members and ex-students, and spent many months doing forensic dives in academic, press and government archives. Simply, something should be done for the forty or so children who still live in the cult in Massachusetts, many of whom are now reportedly home-schooled. It's hard to convey the level of emotional damage and trauma that people who have had childhoods in this group carry with them throughout their lives. Some have what I would describe as storms of sorrow that have to be frequently weathered both consciously and unconsciously. It's even harder to explain how Grenville Christian College and the Community of Jesus managed to fool so many people over so many years while doing so much harm, as many former members/students state. What possessed these supposed Christians to treat children in this way? After all, their own Bible is clear on the fate of anybody who would "offend" a child: "Better for him that a millstone were hanged about his neck, and that he were drowned in the depth of the sea" (Matthew 18:6).

However difficult it has been for plaintiffs to hear the Community of Jesus's expensive Boston lawyer defending the cult in the press during the trial and the CBC's *Fifth Estate* program and denying any connection between the two, there were excellent reasons not to have included the Community of Jesus in that legal action. The reasons the cult was dropped from the suit were purely technical: the difficulty of negotiating two jurisdictions and the new premium in the U.S. over the past decade or so on First Amendment "Religious Freedom" arguments in legal cases. In the U.S., state or federal oversight on minors taken to live in religious communities or cults has historically been very weak and is increasingly embattled by the Evangelical Christian home-schooling movement. Tackling the jurisdictional and political challenges of crossing the border would have meant the case dragging on far, far longer than the twelve years it finally took to get to court. The plaintiffs', or former students', lawyers made the practical choice in their clients' interests to exclude them from the suit.

According to Professor Marshall, paraphrasing the work of Professor Wendy Brown, "Religious freedom entails a sort of contradiction, because no religion in the world has ever endorsed the kind of liberal individual rights and freedoms that are central to American democracy, certainly not the Puritan founders! What religious freedom protects is the right to choose our faith and mode of worship without interference or preferential treatment by the state – that's the basic principle of separation of Church and State, and it is fundamental to democracy. The First Amendment guarantees freedom of religion in the U.S., but certainly not freedom in religion."

I am enough of a libertarian, in the non–U.S. sense of the word, to think that consenting adults in their right minds can join whatever faith or cult they like and even drink the Kool-Aid there. Children, on the other hand, cannot freely choose. We don't grant minors the capacity of consent in cases of sexual violation, so why should society allow them to be subjected to religious indoctrination when it also involves sexual, physical and psychological violence? I now have the scientific confidence to call the Community what I have always felt it to be: a mind-control cult that functions (without outside oversight) through preying on the weak and vulnerable, in service not to God, but rather the greed and/or vanity of its leaders.

The Community of Jesus grew out of what scholars call the Charismatic Movement or Charismatic Renewal, which broke in successive waves over the United States and around the globe beginning in the early 1960s and peaking in the 1980s. The simplest description of it is the adoption by individual Christians across a range of denominations – evangelicals, Episcopalians, Presbyterians, Methodists, even Catholics – of beliefs and practices we typically associate with Pentecostalism. Millions claimed the "gifts of the Holy Spirit," or "charisms" from which the movement got its name: speaking in tongues (glossolalia) and their interpretation, divine healing and other miracles, prophecies and visions, the discernment of the "Spirits." There was an acute focus on the work of Satan (sometimes in almost cartoonish iterations) in the "End Times" as the prospect of Jesus's imminent return created a new sense of urgency about America's coming demise. This urgency hasn't abated much: in a 2010 Pew Research Center survey on trends in U.S. Christianity, 41 percent of Americans reported they expected to see Jesus return by 2050.

The Charismatic Movement in the U.S. took off among mostly

socially and politically conservative white Christians as an explicitly conservative, countercultural movement reacting to the massive socio-cultural and political upheavals of the late 1950s and '60s. Its direct foils were the atheist communist threat, the emergence of a "left-wing" or even "communist" Social Gospel associated with the civil rights and anti-war movements, the women's movement and the landmark 1973 *Roe v. Wade* decision that legalized abortion. Alongside this was the hippie movement's embrace of Christ in the Age of Aquarius – the Jesus freaks, shown in the Broadway musical *Jesus Christ Superstar* from the 1970s. (Unsuprisingly, this musical was still viewed as satanic many years later when I was a young child at the Community of Jesus.)

While claiming to be taking part in the moral and religious defence of a now decadent and degenerate America, these groups were just as concerned about their political and economic values, which had become aligned with Republican interests and ideologies sometime between the 1930s and the '50s – anti–New Deal, pro-business and libertarian. As the era of the televangelist dawned, they began to broadcast highly mythologized visions of America as a white Christian nation since its founding, grounded in supposed "traditional" family values and patriarchal leadership and strict gender roles, setting up what we now call the "culture wars." "God's Own Country" would henceforth require Bible-believing and Holy Spirit–baptized Christians to play a central role in Republican party politics, first through Jerry Falwell Sr.'s Moral Majority, founded around 1979, followed by Pat Robertson's Christian Coalition, founded a few years later.

Cay Andersen and Judy Sorensen were completely caught up in this movement and its major figures. As might be obvious, the Charismatic Movement was very white, very conservative and very Republican in its leanings. It should be no surprise then that the Community of Jesus was and still is almost exclusively white, with very few exceptions. Andersen herself was explicitly racist.

She and Sorensen also dabbled for a while during the '60s and seemingly after in the '70s in an American version or variation of Anglo-Israelism, with a more than somewhat crazy "replacement" heterodoxy that claims in some variations that the Anglo-Saxons are the true "Jews." Post–WWII in the U.S., this movement gave rise to the Christian Identity movement that was more concerned about race.

There is no better statement of this new phase of U.S. white Christian nationalism and exceptionalism than Peter Marshall and David Manuel's Christian revisionist book – you could call a hymn to this mythologized history – *The Light and the Glory: 1492–1793*, first published in 1977 and reprinted several times since. A consistent seller, the book is still very much in print in a new edition. There is even a children's version that continues to sell well. Marshall and Manuel's mythologized account of a Christian American founding has recently been back in the spotlight amongst the new Christian nationalists of the Trump era, along with the grim document *Project 2025*, according to Dr. Marshall. It is also notable that the Charismatic Movement has also been associated with and influenced by Christian Reconstructionism, which is an extreme version of this vision that sees America not just as a Christian nation, but wants a society governed by Biblical law, where Christian institutions govern and regulate social life, and where male family heads or patriarchs have total authority over their wives and children. This would be a society where the state has a limited or non-existent role in education. Does this remind anyone of the similarities to the ancient Roman paterfamilias, which even ancient Rome eventually abolished?

While citing the influence of the *Light and the Glory*, scholars have not realized that David Manuel was among the several "trust-fund babies" who joined the Community near its beginning in the early 1970s (he appears to have deliberately hid this from the outside world), becoming a "star" inside member for his personal wealth, skill set as a non-literary editor and writer, and connections to the broader Charismatic Movement. After a brief stint at Doubleday in the late '60s as an editor of books reportedly on religious esoterica and alien sightings, he quit around 1970, and joined the newly founded Logos International Fellowship, whose call was "to serve the Charismatic Renewal with books on Baptism in the Holy Spirit." He helped Cay and Judy with the cult's publishing wing at the time, Rock Harbor Press, which was a precursor to Paraclete Press.

As the publishing wing of the cult, Paraclete has been very successful in representing itself as a respectable Christian press, sending its glossy brochures to top theology departments across the country, and regularly participating as an exhibitor at the American Academy of Religion's massive annual academic conference. David Manuel remained at the cult, where he reportedly ghostwrote books and indulged in a series of crime novels about a fictional monk, which appeared to be very closely patterned on life at the Community, until a bitter parting with Mother Betty around 2007.

Peter Marshall is the son of the Senate Chaplain of the same name, made famous by his wife, Catherine Marshall LeSourd, a wealthy socialite and Christian author, in her book turned popular movie, *A Man Called Peter*. Peter Jr. was a Presbyterian minister whose parish in East Dennis on Cape Cod was known for its Charismatic services. He was bringing members of his congregation with him to the Community. According to former senior members, at one point, Peter Marshall was the only person famous enough to be allowed to preach with Andersen and Sorensen at retreats or during the weekly Monday night sessions. He is very well known in the wider Charismatic world as the head of Peter Marshall Ministries, which nobody seems to have noticed was run out of the Community of Jesus from the mid to late '70s until he finally broke with them sometime in the '80s. His mother was a visitor at the Community in its very early years, as was Corrie ten

Boom, the famous Dutch evangelist who strongly disagreed with Cay and Judy on many things and broke with them once she discovered they were separating children from their parents.

Catherine Marshall also made a hard break with the Community early on. It is interesting to note that Charles Farnsworth, the future child-abusing headmaster of Grenville Christian College, was also a visitor around this time (1969) and came to Andersen and Sorensen for spiritual advice (even, according to his own account, about moving to Canada and starting with Al Haig, what would become Grenville Christian College [*Life Together*, 1981]). Other illustrious members of the COJ also participated as lesser stars in the constant whirl of retreats and speaking events of these decades. Bill Kanaga joined with his family sometime in the late '70s and built a house at the Community around 1981. He reportedly often spoke at meetings of the Full Gospel Business Men's Fellowship and other events for the Republican business community, as well as being affiliated with the Family, the subject of Jeff Sharlet's 2019 Netflix miniseries. He was living full-time at the Community when he was appointed Chair of the U.S. Chamber of Commerce by Ronald Reagan in 1988. He died about a month after I last spoke with him in 2019 inside the Community. He seemed very frail.

While the Charismatic Movement cast about for an appropriate institutional format beyond the model of the trans-denominational fellowship, Andersen and Sorensen had already found a model for their ecumenical monastic community in Germany from another group that had caught the Charismatic bug sometime in the early 1950s. The Evangelical Sisterhood of Mary (ESM) is a monastic community of German, "Lutheran-inspired" Sisters formed in Darmstadt in 1947, two years after the city was bombed to rubble by the Allies during the war. This source cult followed a sin-drenched, very Pentecostal-style apocalyptic theology, complete with speaking in tongues, prophecies and miracles, deploying seriously heterodox practices, all elaborated by one of its founders, Klara Schlink, who took the name Mother Basilea (Greek for "queen"). Basilea and her partner, Mother Martyria, instructed the Cape Cod Mothers during their extended stays in Darmstadt in 1965, '67, '68 and '69. The self-styled German Mothers also visited the Community on several occasions while Basilea was on one of her many North American tours; she also appeared with the famous Pentecostal preacher Benny Hinn in Toronto in 1970s and at one point had a syndicated show on cable networks across the U.S. until the mid-'90s. Interestingly, Benny Hinn also visited the Sisters in Darmstadt in much more recent times. There are videos of them together in their old chapel in Darmstadt in 2017 on YouTube.

In her prolific published writings and recorded teachings, Basilea sets out what would become the Grenville way of life: "living in the light" (1 John 1:7) through the creation of *Lichtgemeinschaften* – Fellowships in the Light. These were translated from the German for Andersen and Sorensen as "light-sessions" or "light-groups." The translation from German also gave them such "Grenvillisms," as the trial lawyers called them, along with the archaic-sounding sins of rebellion, haughtiness and the like.

Fellowships in the Light were rituals Basilea had devised to purify members of sin. We know the routine by now: the "sinful" Sister was encircled and verbally attacked by the Mothers and her fellow Sisters for her "sins," bringing her back into the light. As at the Community of Jesus and Grenville, sessions could continue, at times for hours (almost always with the threat of violence), until the victim was broken down and sobbing in repentance. Suffering and pain were glorified and demanded; perversely, it both revealed the sinner as a sinner, such that every illness or misfortune was a sign of sin, while also redeeming them, because suffering has the effect of annihilating the self. As two ex-ESM Sisters from Finland explain in their academic writings and book on the Sisterhood: "One could never suffer enough to make up for the abundance of sins, yet this was the goal to which we aspired."

A central proof that a Sister really loved Jesus was her ability to break all social bonds, especially familial. In Basilea's eyes, familial love was idolatry: "[Our] Being 'bound' to family is one of the things which hurts Jesus most. Then He is left out. Then our family becomes our god." Ex-Sisters Riitta Lemmetyinen and Marianne Jansson wrote in *Wenn Mauern fallen*, "Each of us became the object of serious accusations and was wounded in spirit. Each of us experienced the rape of our soul."

Evangelical Sisterhood of Mary, 2019. Courtesy Ewan Whyte.

According to former members, Sisters were organized in a rigid hierarchy, each answerable to their "little Mother" up a chain to Basilea, who was answerable only to God. If Hannah Arendt is right in seeing loneliness as the novelty of twentieth-century totalitarianism, then one doesn't need a direct connection to Nazis to make the case. In her book *I Will Give You the Treasures of Darkness: Discovering God's Promise*, Basilea extolls the redemptive benefits of loneliness: "In the night of loneliness and desolation much is accomplished. Loneliness discharges its deadly poison, killing all soulish selfish love" (40). Or in Andersen and Sorensen's version:

CAY ANDERSEN: The looseness and the immorality in the world today cannot be faced with being loving.

JUDY SORENSEN: We have a tape on it. Why don't you buy it? Why don't you listen to it night and day and get yourself brainwashed?

Basilea gave herself over to a paranoid, self-aggrandizing vision where only she and the Sisters' sufferings might stave off the end of days. She was also deeply influenced by the "prophetic visions" of a Sister who was nicknamed "the Quill." This philosophy was recorded in seven volumes of secret teachings that only the most trusted Sisters could see, called "The Hidden Way." By the 1970s the ESM, which had acquired extensive property and outposts around the world, also began preparing practically for the coming apocalypse: "A select group of Sisters of Mary and Kanaan Franciscan Brothers began to hide, to bury and to wall off large quantities, not only of food supplies and Mother Basilea's literature, but of just about everything imaginable. All over Europe and possibly further afield, goods valued in the millions of dollars were hidden away" (86).

Basilea warned the Sisters that they needed to be ready to act in the coming battle with Satan. Interestingly, there was still some contact between the two groups in the late '70s and '80s. The ESM even unsuccessfully negotiated the purchase of bulk dried goods from one of Judy's children, who was running a wholesale dried goods business out of the Community of Jesus, and Sorensen herself claimed she went to Germany after Andersen's death in 1988.

This was how two 1950s housewives, with little in the way of higher education and even less in scriptural knowledge, came up with their idea for the Community of Jesus and ruled over it with the iron hand of totalitarian despots, imposing ego-destroying light-sessions and demanding total, unthinking obedience as the Community and Grenville "way of life." They took Basilea's teachings and techniques and applied them not to a group of dedicated adult women and men, which is bad enough, but to families with children, and then some 1,300 adolescents and children at Grenville Christian College.

One seriously wonders if the horrors perpetrated at Grenville all started because of an extreme form of Christian sexual repression and guilt and an abiding problem with relationships and men. Ex-members emphasize how men were especially targeted and emasculated by the Mothers, and many left their wives behind when they left the Community. Andersen and Sorensen also had a stable of male clergy who were totally under their thumb, including Al Haig and Charles Farnsworth, as well as a one-time Episcopalian, Father Arthur Lane – one of the older Sorensen sons jokingly referred to them as the "Court of Eunuchs." It seems an obvious source for these elaborate edifices built on sin and suffering, these perverse matriarchies where women assumed total charismatic authority in order to reinforce extreme patriarchal social norms, while engaging in the sort of highly eroticized mysticism of sixteenth- and seventeenth-century Catholic women saints.

Both Basilea and Andersen were enamoured of the mystic St. Teresa d'Avilà. One ex–ESM Sister characterized Basilea's "Way" as a combination of elements from pre–Vatican II Catholicism, a Pentecostal focus on the Holy Spirit in the End Times and a large body of "homegrown" ideas taken from "the Quill's repressed homo-erotic visions." They continually railed against homosexuals, saying they could "feel it in the Spirit" if one ever walked onto the property.

Farnsworth took the Mothers' Christian sexual repression and guilt complex to an extreme level. Both Joan Childs, member of the at one time four-person leadership team at Grenville, and Margit Mayberry, a long-time teacher there, testified at the trial in the same bald terms: Charles was obsessed with sex. As was also revealed in two one-hour *Fifth Estate* documentaries (2021 and 2022) and a *W5* news exposé (2016), Farnsworth preyed sexually on students.

In addition to the harrowing testimony of a representative plaintiff in the Grenville trial, who recounts being constantly "slut-shamed" by him, as well as being quizzed on her sexual fantasies at age fifteen, a paying student recounted on the stand how he was body shamed and light-sessioned for being "effeminate" and a "faggot" while naked in the shower. Another paying student testified about having the "gay" prayed out of him by a "group laying on of hands" on his naked penis.

Teenaged girls were paddled on their bare asses by men. Dan Ortolani, member of the inner circle, took a peculiar enjoyment from beating children. I recall his sadism from my time there, as does David Ardill: "Ortolani was just a psychopath." Farnsworth was endlessly on the lookout for sexual sins and had a whole network of informants in the staff as well as the prefects, and other favoured and compliant students. As many plaintiffs testified, he saw women as evil temptresses responsible for exciting sinful lust in boys, and no doubt, in himself. If a girl was raped, well, in Anglican priest and Grenville headmaster Charles Farnsworth's view, she'd asked for it.

The ridiculous dress code for girls, and the "six-inch rule" were the least troubling aspects of his perverse obsession. Several women have had the courage to tell me about their horrifying personal experiences with Farnsworth. One recounted how she had been sexually abused by an older girl in the dorm when she was fourteen and that Farnsworth got wind of this. As they entered his office to be "disciplined," they found him sitting behind his desk. He made the girls sit on chairs he'd placed in front of the desk with their backs to him. He then instructed them to recount in elaborate detail what had gone on between them, making them pause and repeat often, pressing for details, asking each one how it made her feel. Another student was sixteen when Farnsworth invited her to his summer cottage with his family. She woke up from a nap to find him on top of her, groping and kissing her.

Another former student's story is starker: "I was sexually abused by Charles Farnsworth when I was a student in the elementary school at Grenville Christian College. I was also a staff kid at the time. And it had, continues to have, a lasting and profound impact on my life and on my sense of self." This student doesn't remember how Farnsworth's actions became known among the staff, and much later, after Charles had retired, she tells me, "Grenville admins, in a letter to the Bishop in Kingston, wrote about the possibility that 'a child of some Grenville staff might go forward with accusations of sexual abuse against Charles Farnsworth. And what would they do about it if that happened?' I don't really know how those people came to know about it. But I do know that Joan Childs talked to Betty Pugsley about it and said there's no way this could have happened and someone in authority said, 'I wouldn't be so sure about that.'" One wonders how long those in authority and Betty might had held this view of their spiritual charge.

Anglican Bishop Allan Read blessing a student in a formal service at Grenville Christian College, 1992. Grenville Christian College yearbook, 1991–1992.

Farnsworth, under the spiritual authority of Andersen, Sorensen and Pugsley, learned to follow their lead in ensuring he was surrounded by legitimators, acolytes, powerful patrons and supporters. The Anglican Church in Canada served this purpose wonderfully, as did the many illustrious, wealthy families who sent their children there, along with a who's who of throwbacks to the Family Compact of Upper

Canada, who sat on the school's board, attended lavish dinners and gave commencement speeches over the years. Sir Arthur and Lady Marjory Chetwynd were powerful promoters and introduced many others to the school.

Al Haig, Grenville's first headmaster and a University of Toronto alum, recounts in his autobiography – published by a Community of Jesus–associated press – that his wife, Mary, had also seen "The Cay and Judy Show" in Toronto, along with a number of other upper-middle-class housewives, who would later send their children there.

More shocking is how the school billed itself as Anglican in all its promotional literature and to many wealthy prospective parents, raising the Anglican flag and receiving regular visits from the bishops in Kingston, while really being nothing of the sort. The bishop in Kingston who oversaw the diocese, Bishop Henry Hill, visited the Community for retreats and (as claimed in court) may have actually taken oblate member vows of obedience to the Mothers. This might help explain the fact that he ordained Charles Farnsworth, in a bizarre, fast-tracked fashion in 1977, despite him never having been to a seminary or university. The Anglican Church's lawyers worked very hard to make sure the Church was not named as a defendant in the Class Action.

The Anglican Church of Canada cannot say it was unaware of what was going on – it was committed by two of their ordained priests, and sanctioned by their own bishop, who had reportedly vowed obedience to the Mothers. David Ardill, a paying student who was beaten by Ortolani and Charles Farnsworth several different times in his first three months at Grenville, until he ran away, explains:

> It was all disguised. I don't think I would have been sent there, my mother was a straitlaced Anglican. She wouldn't have sent me to some crazy cult school. It was all because

it was sanctioned by the Anglican Church. They flew the Anglican flag. They read from the Anglican book, wore the Anglican garb. For the Anglican Church to turn around now and say, "Well, no, it wasn't us; It was you! You know you were the ones that sanctioned it" . . . One thing I'm angry about is the Church has been separated from it, and I think they're as responsible as anybody. They knew what was going on. The OPP knew what was going on.

Even more shocking is another student's story. His family is Jewish, and his parents were promised he would not have to participate in the school's religious instruction. Not only were no students exempted from attending chapel, they were all also subjected to the endless extemporaneous exhortations, public light-sessions, boys' dorm sessions with Farnsworth and sermons over meals. However, Farnsworth went further with this potential convert. During his only year at Grenville in Grade 10, he was submitted to such intense light-sessions and indoctrination by Farnsworth that when he returned home at the end of the year, he announced to his family that they were going to burn in hell as unbelievers, and that his grandmother, mother and sister were "sluts." Appalled, his parents pulled him from the school against his will – he desperately wanted to return to Grenville and then become a monk at the Community. He was fifteen, and only there for one year, but this brainwashing broke him and deeply affected his adult life.

Since the school's closure and even the trial, the Anglican Diocese of Ontario has nonetheless ordained and promoted two ex-teachers and administrators: Gordon Mintz as an Anglican priest and Julia Case in some lay capacity. Donald Farnsworth, Charles's son and the main defendant in the class-action suit, claimed to be undertaking a Divinity degree at Wycliffe College, at the University of Toronto, professing his intent to join the priesthood as well. It's staggering to think that any church would ordain and promote individuals who continue to defend Grenville and deny the abuse confirmed by so many dozens of class members who testified or submitted statements. How is it possible that pastoral charges of any kind be given to people who not only have sworn lifetime vows to a cult and its leaders, but have been accused by dozens of students of running an institution whose hallmark was the physical, sexual and psychological abuse of children?

The Anglicans are in good company these days I suppose, given the scandals rocking the Catholic Church over widespread child sexual abuse. We met one of theirs in Florence, Monsignor Timothy Verdon, Canon of Florence's famous medieval Duomo, the Santa Maria del Fiore Cathedral. With a PhD in Art History from Yale, according to his personal website, Verdon was Consultant to the Pontifical Commission for the Cultural Heritage of the Church, a Fellow of the Harvard University Center for Italian Renaissance Studies (Villa I Tatti) and at the time of writing teaches in the Florence Program of Stanford University. Monsignor Verdon is also Director of the Mount Tabor Ecumenical Centre for Art and Spirituality, the cult's luxurious holiday villa in the charming walled Tuscan hill village of Barga, Italy. He also has several works published by

Community of Jesus mansion, Mount Tabor Ecumenical Centre for Art & Spirituality, Barga, Italy. Courtesy Ewan Whyte.

Paraclete Press, and his picture features on the press's website.

Dr. Ruth Marshall and I visited the "centre" in Barga – a massive centuries-old villa situated on a high hill in the town, lavishly renovated and updated to the highest standards – and conversed with a Brother and Sister there. The Brother, who must have been in his late fifties, told us he'd attended Grenville Christian College, but claimed that it had no connection at all to the Community of Jesus, even as he told us that we had to meet Mary Haig, fellow Torontonian, at the Community of Jesus. It transpired that the only art on show at this "arts and spirituality centre" had been closed for many months. It had consisted of an exhibition, in a small lower room, of artwork done by a long-time Community member, together with some sort of assistant to Verdon who was listed as Artistic Director of the Centre.

The two told us that art wasn't actually done at the centre, nor did they have regular visits or tours, though the Brother went into great detail describing for us the construction of the Community's impressive Church of the Transfiguration begun in the 1990s and completed over several years (and dedicated in 2000) under Mother Betty's direction, which is showcased in the villa. Incredibly, it's a medieval basilica built almost to scale about 350 metres from the water's edge on Rock Harbor. He spoke about the role of Italian artists and craftsmen in its incredibly lavish, if rather kitsch, interior decoration. The organ is a particular point of pride, as one of the largest in North America. From the 1990s on, the focus on art and music and the Vatican appears to be the vanity project of Betty Pugsley. At the time of writing, the Paraclete Press extolled "the ecumenical charism of the Community and its dedication to sacred music, the fine arts, and the written word." Betty took over the direction of the choir from her husband, when he was sent away to Cambridge, England, sometime in the 1990s, a few years after Andersen died in 1988. Rick Pugsley Sr.'s banishment followed a scandal where some were prepared to press charges against him for sexually assaulting their sons, some who were not yet in high school. I have already mentioned having my body parts groped by him while in the choir as a child there. There were numerous incidents of other members sexually assaulting children in the Community of Jesus. Some of the sexual assaults on children in the Community of Jesus perpetrated by another man were reported by the CBC in its *Fifth Estate* episode "School of Secrets" (2022). Unfortunately, there were others. In that program a woman is interviewed who claims to have been sexually assaulted by Charles Farnsworth at the Community of Jesus in the same room as another boy, who backs up her story. This first-person account is upsetting to watch. There was a text exchange included in the program with Don Farnsworth and the sex assault victim that seems to imply Don Farnsworth thought it might be true.

No charges it seems were laid by the Orleans police department.

Dr. Marshall and I met with Monsignor Verdon inside the Duomo of Florence after attending Vespers he officiated, and in this surreal setting, told him about our research in order to warn him that the people he was working with were not who they appeared. I told him about my experiences and my diagnosis of Complex Post-Traumatic Stress Disorder and showed him a series of affidavits from ex-Community kids and Grenville students, as well as David Manuel's correspondence. I told him about adult Community of Jesus members sexually abusing children inside the compound. At first, he appeared very shocked and willing to believe us. I shared David Manuel's 2008 affidavit with him at this point, drawing his attention to the section where Manuel confirms that Pugsley made advances to the boys in the choir:

> Another person in that circle who was not practicing celibacy was Rick Pugsley, who was director of music at that time.

It came to Barbara's and my attention that sometime in the 1990's he had used his position to make sexual advances towards some of the young men to whom he was giving voice lessons.

However, over the course of the conversation, perhaps realizing what a pickle he was now in, he became increasingly hostile. When we suggested that the Community was very good at keeping up appearances, he responded, "I have seen them not only in action in their own place but in context here and indeed I introduced them to very important people in the Church in Italy, all of whom remain deeply impressed by them, and so what you call manipulation comes across to us here as real sincerity . . . I have the impression that what you're saying is true, I simply can't relate it to the people that I've met. And I'm not sure I should."

When I asked him what he thought about their artwork, he was surprised by the question, even though I had told him I was an art writer, but agreed with me that it was kitsch: "The usual failing in this effort is to try to go in one or another direction toward the past. You come up with something that is either réchauffé or kitsch. That's an almost inevitable hole in the road, as it were."

I asked him if he would continue working with the cult, now that we had spoken with him and showed him our documents. We pointed out that Dr. Marshall has thirty years of expertise and that we were sure of our facts, and we had thought it in his interest to know. He responded, "Certainly, if there's going to be a big scandal, thank you, it's in my interests to be forewarned. I don't know what to do. As I say, I don't see any concrete reason to suddenly . . . what am I supposed to do, publish an article saying, 'I repudiate my relationship with the Community of Jesus'?"

When we replied we didn't know what he should do, he became hostile and raised his voice: "Is this just another paragraph in the book, you approached someone who works with the Community of Jesus, and he gave you these answers? Disappear!" I responded with "Thank you very much" and extended my hand toward him. He answered, "I'm not going to do that. I'm not going to shake your hand."

Later that night he wrote a hostile email to Dr. Marshall, and copied both the cult's lawyers. It was surprising to be treated as a liar and rebuffed so aggressively by a man with his authority. But given my experience with all levels of religious governance and their ability to turn a blind eye while blaming the victims, it didn't come as a surprise.

We returned home and went back to Brockville to walk around the old Grenville grounds, until we were threatened by one of its extremely unpleasant overseers at the time, whom I later learned is a supposed friend of the Farnsworths. This might explain his hostility when I told him I was an ex-student. He went on an extended rant about how great Grenville had been as a school and complained bitterly about the *W5* investigative crew and host Victor Malarek. He made a series of totally false allegations against Malarek and his crew and claimed he'd been bullied and victimized by the

A view of the central courtyard of the Community of Jesus compound, 2019. Courtesy Ewan Whyte.

ex-students, and then threatened me with police action and said he was a former police officer.

I also somehow went back two more times into the Community with Dr. Marshall, where we joined a tour of their basilica, heard an organ demonstration, went to a Vespers service and chatted with members in their gift shop, accompanied on one occasion by a Nigerian friend and colleague, Professor Nimi Wariboko, the Walter G. Muelder Chair of Social Ethics at Boston University, who has also worked for decades on Pentecostals and Charismatics. I saw Mary Haig (now Mary Haig French) on each occasion; she was friendly and effusive and even offered to organize a retreat for the "Professors" if they wanted to learn more. I was stunned that nobody recognized me.

Our last visit to the Community of Jesus on June 21, 2019, ended when a long-time member called the police on us. Flanked by two police officers, he issued threats about seeing us in court simply because I had openly and legally pulled out my recorder in the gift shop and told them I was recording myself and that they did not have to speak. It had turned into an eight-minute discussion with a Brother and Sister, whom I remembered well, about my experiences at the Community of Jesus as a child. There was nothing disorderly about the exchange; in fact, the Brother offered me a qualified apology, the only one I expect I'll ever get from the cult.

> EWAN WHYTE: When I was a child I was here at the Community of Jesus. As a small child, at age ten, I was forced to eat my own vomit by in the house that you called Judea. And it was utterly devastating experience, and when I think of the children . . . It kept on going on – light-sessions . . . I was pushed down the stairs by [name redacted, an adult member of the Community] and I had damaged vertebrae to my neck . . . You don't have to say anything.

[. . .]

BROTHER: I'm not challenging anything you're saying, I'm not countering it, I'm not accusing you of anything that's wrong that you're saying. I'm very, very sorry if that ever happened. It's not for me to apologize, but obviously it was an extremely damaging and extremely unfortunate, terrible thing and I don't know what else to say. I mean, I'm . . . I'm grieved that that happened.

SISTER: And we pray for your healing. We certainly understand.

BROTHER: That's not what we're about.

WHYTE: I'm shocked. You are a very different Brother from the Brother I knew when I was a child.

BROTHER: Well I'm glad to hear that. That's a positive.

WHYTE: You've grown. I mean, not in height. I'm shocked, I'm really shocked actually.

BROTHER: Let's hope that, let's hope that the rest of us have grown too.

We did end up in court on criminal charges of disorderly conduct, thanks it seems to the clout of a powerful member and the cult, which apparently extends to police and judicial corruption. Not only did the cult members lie about the interaction on their written statements, but the police officers seem to have lied on their statements as well. They also seem to have lied in email to Dr. Marshall when she queried the legality of the cult's audiovisual recording, which the police at the scene had told us they were viewing with the long-time member while we waited outside. While I followed Massachusetts dual-consent recording laws, the cult, which has had CC video surveillance everywhere since the '80s, evidently records patrons in their gift shop without their knowledge or consent. There were no displayed signs of this anywhere, as is the law as I understand it.

Trumped-up charges didn't surprise me, as this cult, founded by the rich and famous, has done what it likes in this small Cape Cod town for fifty years with total impunity. Children who ran away would regularly be brought back by police, and despite receiving reports of abuse over decades, local law enforcement and school authorities have done nothing. My personal account of this when I was ten and attending the local Orleans school is beyond shocking. Even as a little kid, I came to realize that the police were not going to help me, no one would.

Judge Welch III in Barnstable County wasn't willing to give the cult the trial it was pushing for, saying there was no basis in law for the charges of disorderly conduct in the first place: "The defendants simply confronted several individuals about their grievances within their free speech rights and then when asked to leave they left."

Intimidation is what the cult does best, not just to its members, but to its potential detractors. The lawyers also sent two libellous letters to the president of the University of Toronto, trying to stop Dr. Marshall from helping me with the research and have her sanctioned. One of these letters included as an attachment a private document our attorney had prepared for the trial that could only have been obtained illegally. For a group that claims it has nothing to reproach itself for, these sorts of extreme litigious actions, threats and corruption are hard to fathom. Their lawyer is on record speaking for the cult in the *Cape Cod Times* on March 9, 2020, where he dismisses my allegations against the community: "This is the sort of garbage that has been peddled unsuccessfully every once in a while."

I suppose after decades of abusing, lying and threatening with impunity, one gets the impression one is invincible. It's hard to say whether this is hubris or not in the present moment. It may be the era of Catholic child abuse scandals, #MeToo and Black Lives Matter, but it is also a world turned upside down by a series of potentially devastating plagues: Covid-19, the more extremes of Trumpism and white supremacy, the global rise of right-wing populist authoritarians and the dangerous hyper-deliria of the fanatically religious at home, not just abroad.

Landscapes from the Back of a Train

A Personal Essay of the Memory of a Cult Childhood

I

My imagination carries my sight through the kaleidoscopic distance, falling away from what was a moment ago. Trees, bridges, water and the changing animal clouds in the sky shift with the lights at the sides of the tracks and overpasses that temporarily mark all changing lines of sight.

After dark, the stars move back and forth over the train through leafless branches, dragging Orion's feet through the top of the forest. Later Sirius is running through the trees shaking along the rails through my imagination to the opposing train's violent approach and passing. A harbinger of anticipation of a coming destination, a likely final meeting in the consciousness of memory.

II

It had been a number of years since I had last seen my mother. I heard that she was not well, that she was having memory problems. When I would speak with her on the phone she seemed to be mentally declining but tried very hard to hide it. This autumn I travel the distance through New York to Beaufort on the South Carolina coast to visit my ailing mother. It is a long train ride. We do not choose our parents or our genes. These are just presented to us. I was hoping there would be enough left of her to say goodbye to. Goodbye to an emotionally injured mother. We all love our mothers, even if they have behaved badly.

III

She was born in North Carolina shortly before the Second World War. She had had a difficult life. Her mother suddenly died around her twelfth birthday. Her father was very sick and in and out of hospital at the time. She was sent to live with others. Her chronically ill father died four years later. The last time I had seen her, she shocked me by telling me that she was repeatedly raped over several years during this time. She eventually moved to New England and refused any activity outside her studies with the sole exception of going to church. She received her MA in Education from Boston University as Valedictorian of her graduating class in her mid-twenties. She then started a life of sporadic teaching and frequent attendance in very conservative religious groups. She married an equally emotionally damaged man and became a mother.

When I think of her through the sound of the rails at the back of the train, I think of her in the comforting rhythm of loud calming white noise, its repeating patterning sounds to the changing landscape.

I have come to forgive her.

IV

When I was eight years old, she joined an extreme mind-control sect on Cape Cod in Massachusetts, called the Community of Jesus. The compound included roughly fifteen houses and had about two hundred and fifty members. She dropped me off at its compound for the summer that year in the late '70s. My immediate reception was hostile and within five minutes I was threatened with violence and laughed at by adult members. It was strange to suddenly be in a place for the whole summer where I had no friends. There were bunk beds crowded into each small bedroom to house the changing number of roughly ten to twenty children.

I was not allowed to see my parents, except for a few times, for very short member-supervised meetings, or have contact with anyone from the outside world. Beating of children by anonymous adult cult members was a constant threat and sometimes we would go to sleep at night through the screams of other children being beaten.

We were subjected daily to a severe brainwashing technique called a "light-session" that would often go on for hours, during which adults would scream at an individual, insulting their very being from point-blank range for trivial things or imagined sins of the spirit. There was a specific technique during a light-session called "blasting," where the adult would put their face immediately in front of the child's face, almost touching it, and scream as loudly as they could. The individual would always give in and admit to whatever completely imagined sin they were accused of, often very quickly, especially if they were a young child or teenager, where physical violence was always a significant possibility. The purpose I learned later was to break our spirits and to eventually make us become adult members of this sect.

I dealt with this very hostile situation through secret escape into my own imagination. The scraps of poetry I had memorized from books became my friends, although I would sometimes get the lines wrong. There were almost no books at the compound and the very few there were, we had no access to. We were forced to work for free, from early morning till around 4:00 p.m. every day except Sunday in the vegetable gardens and grounds of the compound.

When I eventually saw my mother after over a month, I pleaded with her to let me leave. She told me it was a special place that was blessed by God. She told the adult members that I was complaining and should be punished. She then left me alone there for the rest of that summer.

The situation got worse. She became a devoted member of the Community of Jesus and I was moved there permanently before I was ten and stayed, rarely seeing my parents until I was eleven when

I moved to Canada with them. My mother and father maintained their involvement with this cult and I was forced to continue living its extreme interrogation lifestyle, returning to the Community of Jesus each year for the summer.

As well as being forced to take part in "light-groups for light-sessions" with Community of Jesus members at the cult's affiliate (where sworn members of the Community of Jesus ran) Grenville Christian College in Brockville, Ontario, I was later forced to attend Grenville Christian College boarding school, for three very abusive years where it was understood that if I escaped, the police would bring me back, as they did to so many other children and teenagers. The boarding school was run by sworn avowed members of the Community of Jesus. During this time, my mother was a devoted follower and teacher there. She, along with the other cult members, forced visits to the Community of Jesus every summer until I was legally able to leave, when I went down for a final confrontation with them before leaving for good.

V

Self-styled Mothers Cay Andersen and Judy Sorensen, the leaders of the Community of Jesus, had visited other self-styled Mothers in Germany, who earlier had set up their own sect in Darmstadt called the Evangelical Sisterhood of Mary in 1947. The two Mothers from Germany gave themselves the names Mother Basilea and Mother Martyria, and appeared to be Lutheran-based originally. They were obsessed with German guilt over the Second World War and they wanted to employ the same techniques used by Germans during the war but for the good of pointing out German guilt.

Mother Basilea had a PhD in psychology and seems to have used her knowledge to considerable effect. The website of the Evangelical Sisterhood of Mary states: "God commissioned our two spiritual mothers to build a chapel where he would receive honour and worship. As confirmation they received the following scripture: 'Let them make me a sanctuary that I may dwell among them'" (Exodus 25:8). Their group has been described and referred to as cult-like in European academic writing. One in particular is from a very highly regarded German University.

Here are excerpts from a piece originally written in German, titled, *Eine ehemalige Marienschwester erzählt ihre Geschichte* in 2007, by Charlene Andersen about her fourteen years as a member of the Evangelical Sisterhood of Mary in Darmstadt (she left in 1999):

> And Mother Basilea took over the lead to the community and also the lead of the "Lichtgemeinschaften" on the basis of Johannes 1.9. [If we confess our sins, he is faithful and just and will forgive us our sins and purify us from all unrighteousness.]
>
> These "Lichtgemeinschaften" meetings were meant to cleanse the Sisters from all evils." ["Licht" means "light," "gemeinschaften" means "communities" – so it means "Communities of Light."]
>
> And this is how the "Lichtgemeinschaften" were carried out: one Sister after another had to confess which of their own words and deeds had harmed the community. While [one Sister] was standing there, everybody who found something sinful in the standing Sister, was invited to speak . . .
>
> The "Lichtgemeinschaften" meeting took hours and it happened often that the Sisters who were criticized a lot broke down, cried and condemned themselves . . . During these meetings it was not allowed to justify oneself. One had to act quietly and subservient and to humiliate oneself . . .
>
> I think the terrors of these meetings I have never overcome. Instead of creating harmony and healing within the community these meetings created, to my view, mistrust and fear . . . My description will be eventually a warning for the subtle power of spiritual seduction.

The ones among you who have never been a member of a sect will have challenges to understand what I am talking about. [She uses the German word "sekte" but it arguably could also be translated as "cult" – it appears to be a much stronger word than the English "sect."]

There may be a link between Nazi interrogation techniques and this group. Peter Andersen, son of Mother Cay, stated:

> Both of the German mothers spent months at Rock Harbor [the Community of Jesus] on Cape Cod to teach Cay and Judy how to set up a monastic community and most importantly, how to perform light-sessions, which they called a "Monastic Discipline." Cay and Judy's version was brutal beyond what was practiced in Germany. Charles Farnsworth later, under Cay and Judy's influence, imported them to use on children at Grenville. The institutional foundations are from the practices of that order in Germany, and Basilea was influenced by her parents who were [according to some of those who knew them and her as] ardent National Socialists during the war.

According to Peter Andersen, Cay said: "We're going to do this 'community thing' better. We can do better than these people."

VI

A *Globe and Mail* article from 2007 stated that Mother Judy started having a sexual affair with one of the nuns from the sect in Germany. (That was hypocritical as we were told at the Community of Jesus that if anyone gay stepped on the property, the Mothers would feel it in the Spirit of God.) After this, all the women were called back to Germany for serious correction.

It was on the basis of the very harsh mind-control light-sessions lifestyle that the Community of Jesus was organized and controlled. Its leaders managed to live lives of luxury with a private plane and an estate in Bermuda, while so many of those of the low ranks and young children suffered. A United Church of Christ USA minister wrote this about life at the Community of Jesus cult and Grenville Christian College in 2007: "The children of community members were dealt with in a strict and often harsh manner. My son was ten when we lived in the Community in separate homes as was the policy. He was forced to eat all his food and on several occasions was forced to eat his vomit after he had thrown up."

Growing up in a hostile environment, isolated and without emotional or practical family support, was difficult. As a child it was hard to get over the sickening level of abuse that just got worse and worse. The far-reaching after-effects of this were much more significant than I initially realized.

VII

I ended up homeless in my twenties, sleeping on public benches in parks during the day as it was too dangerous to try to sleep at night. I had my consuming interest in writing and memorizing poetry. Even in the roughest of circumstances it was always some form of comfort. When you are suffering Homer is still great poetry, despite edging on parody from time to time. Odysseus in *The Odyssey*, "And then he beat his breast and cried, be strong my heart, far worse have you endured."

VIII

My mother remained an ardent supporter of the cult till the very end of her mind. Oddly, she did not seem surprised that eventually there were legal proceedings and criminal investigations against the group, with many pages of shocking affidavits. From what I can surmise from her behaviour, it appears she adhered to this cult as it related to something in her that was lost in her years of sexual abuse; and with the same intensity as she felt her emotional wounds she clung to this cult. She claimed to be tithing part of her income and she told me she signed papers of loyalty to them for life.

Well I forgive her anyways; a person has to be very ill to treat their own child in that way. In the end, I have come to realize, it was actually about her and not about me.

IX

My first evening visiting my mother in her home, at her insistence, we watched a nature documentary together. It was focused around a mother hippo and a baby hippo in a central African lake. Presented with commentary, a baby hippo was beside its mother when a large crocodile came near. The mother was alert and looked menacing. The crocodile swam away. The baby moves immediately beside its mother. It knows it is in danger but soon forgets after its mother eases her guard. It swims around looking at the fish in an almost ballet-like display from an underwater camera and gets so engrossed at what it is doing that it gets further and further away from its mother, who does not follow. She does not call to the baby hippo.

The camera showed a crocodile swimming along slowly behind, tracking it. The little hippo continues in playful moments of seeming joy and delight in the world of colourful fish around it. When the baby hippo finally notices the crocodile behind it, the crocodile is quite close. The small hippo creeps to the side of the lake but is trapped by dense reeds and cannot escape. The crocodile moves close. The mother just watches from a distance.

The crocodile pauses a moment, looks at the mother hippo, who does not move, then at the baby hippo, who has given up and is looking scared, accepting its fate. The crocodile moves in casually without the speed it is known for. It snaps its jaws down hard on the baby hippo, killing it in one bite. It slides back and watches the body floating for a few seconds before coming back and dragging it away under the water. Like a reality show, there is a camera shot on the mother, who looks almost humanly sad.

My mother was quite upset by this. She used to like happier ending nature shows.

X

As a child I would often look at older people and think that this had been their personality, their demeanour, their character throughout their entire lives. As teenagers, we realize it is only part of them. Even vicious dictators can descend into dopey kindness and remarkable calm when the situation calls for it.

I did not know what to expect seeing my mother after three years. There was another time when I saw her at the airport and was shocked at how she had changed, at how old she had become. I had travelled a long distance to tell my mother who can no longer remember well or perhaps fully understand that I forgive her.

I find it sad that she is not the same woman who attended the University of North Carolina, Boston University and classes at Harvard. She is not the self-involved woman who would argue about the American nineteenth-century novel before going to her cult meeting where she would usually be the only educated person in the room. She was not the same woman who would go out of her way to teach poorly performing students while giving gifted students a hard time.

I did not spend that much time with my mother, so in some ways I did not really know her in the way that many other children know their parents. But I see her on her back steps, again and again, playing with the kittens that her outdoor cat keeps having, and holding them in her arms like a small child, admiring them, comforted by them, far more than I have ever seen her comforted by people. Perhaps this is a good thing.

She asked me about my poetry. Have I been writing it? She must have remembered it from years ago. She used to ask me to write her a poem. For years I could not write her anything. Now finally I had written her a poem on one of her favourite saints (despite having no belief in her god), St. Francis of Assisi, who was born wealthy and after a dissolute youth gave away all his possessions and wandered out of his town singing. She used to talk about him when I was a small child. She asks me to recite it to her and I did.

Fioretti (of St. Francis)
Returning home
after a wealthy party
stopping for shelter
in a half-fallen country chapel
looking out over the fields
through the holes in the walls
he took off his rich clothes.
For a week he spoke with sister moon
and brother sun,
hearing their songs in inflected light.
After the last night at the first
moments of dawn
when the sun sends its sheets of fire
over the living surface of the earth
he woke with joy and shuddered
to the opening of the fields of flowers.

She says again that she loved St. Francis and she says she likes her poem. She speaks of medieval saint stories. We agree to go for a long walk on the Hunting Island beach in the state park the following morning.

XI
At the beach she asked me to turn on my recorder – she must have remembered I had carried one around for years – as we walk along the sand with her old fellow teacher friend.

EWAN: You have always liked playing with plants.

MOTHER: Oh I like them . . . earthbound . . . [*laughs*] you don't agree?

EWAN: Oh yes.

MOTHER: Just standing here and looking at the beautiful trees it's lovely.

[Huge branches, Spanish moss, twisting to an imagined heaven.]

MOTHER: I do like looking at the trees.

[Their thick gnarled branches under a smooth green canopy.]

[Now picking up giant pine cones from our walk on the beach, gathering shells.]

MOTHER: This one in the middle . . . but it's a pretty one I think . . . don't you want it? It's yours if you don't want it.

[Now on from every side, some of them, it seems, as big as my head.]

I look at her form now as she is walking ahead of me. She looks like an aging ghost, her long grey dress fluttering around her. It hurts to see her like this.

One of the remarkable things about talking to those who have caused significant suffering to others is often discovering their incredible ability to deny anything ever happened. Is it that on one level they don't care and any sense of prevailing justice is for saccharinely comforting Hollywood movies or children's books? It is a stark reality. Asking someone to deny their own emotionally charged lie for another's truth – sometimes it seems like it is almost bordering on arrogance.

She starts visiting with her friend on a bench near the lighthouse and says she will stay seated on the bench. She tells me that she knows I wanted to go up to the top of the famous one-hundred-and-fifty-year-old Hunting Island Lighthouse. I wonder if it's because she remembers or because she almost knows me.

The 167 iron steps to the top of the lighthouse provoke imagination to run with its history. Ships from the Civil War blockade came within sight of this light. It has been fifteen years since I first came here. Now there are two boats miles out, pushing themselves across the sea, frozen in the sea with small white wakes behind them, though they seem utterly still.

Inland in the other direction, trees, birdsongs, deer tracks and the promise of alligators continue in their impersonal task of being; turning back, the ships no farther out, struggle against the day and press on.

XII

And my Alzheimer's-affected mother with her rehashed memory replaying again and again experiences from many years before, still remembering, now confused, in fragments. I wonder where it all goes, memory, steadily falling away. We are on former Cherokee Native land but they have been nearly expunged from remembrance here.

The clouds recycle into new shapes: one looks like a mushroom, which my imagination thinks is running away with words that my present watery clasp of language fails to grasp. The echoing lighthouse chamber from below lifts voices up from the ground; porpoises are jumping out of the water, a pelican is eating an oversized fish and looks like Groucho Marx swallowing a giant pickle whole.

XIII

She is still wearing the membership ring of the cult: a broad flat band in gold with a negative Jerusalem-style cross stamped out of it. Sitting on a bench beside her, looking at that membership ring, I tell her I forgive her.

Because of the years of mind-control light-sessions, in which members' supposed dark intentions were interrogated ad nauseam, individuals sometimes no longer have access to their own personal emotions. My words to her seem to have little meaning, but that's okay. She looks at me in silence this time.

XIV

"Ever since you were a child you used to wonder how much a tree would like to walk," I say. Often she would talk about this passage from Mark 8:23–24: "And he took the blind man by the hand, and led him out of the town; and when he had spit on his eyes, and put his hands upon him, he asked him if he saw anything. And he looked up, and said, '"I see men as trees, walking."'"

MOTHER: Yes.

EWAN: And what would it do when it was walking?

MOTHER: I don't know what it would do, I just don't know, I just would play that the tree was walking over here or over there or whatever, because I was an only child and I had to make my own playmates.

EWAN: Would the trees talk?

MOTHER: Sure, they talked. If any of them made any noise I took it for speech. I guess the squirrels were in their hair. It was a nice big backyard when I was a child and I enjoyed it . . . I enjoyed the critters. My mother had some fits when I brought some wounded critters, it was a fiasco. She would say: "Don't you bring any more critters home. Your father's sick and in the bed." And he was.

[A cat comes close; she leans to pet it.]

MOTHER: We have one like you at home. Bless your little heart.

Notes

"Fioretti" has references to the medieval poem the "Canticle of the Sun" once attributed to St. Francis but now considered a later work, as well as a prayer by the late nineteenth- and early twentieth-century Saint Teilhard de Chardin.

Acknowledgements

Thank you to Noelle and everyone at Wolsak and Wynn.

Thank you to everyone who helped with research or in any way.

Notes

The introduction was published in an earlier version as "The former students of Grenville Christian College have finally found closure" in the *Globe & Mail*, December 9, 2023.

"The Cult that Raised Me" was first published in *Toronto Life* magazine, January 5, 2021.

An earlier version of "The Art of Deception: The Arts, Music and Poetry of the Community of Jesus and Grenville Christian College" was first published in *Shifting Paradigms: Essays on Art and Culture*, Guernica Editions, 2021.

"Landscapes from the Back of a Train" first appeared in *Polska* magazine.

Ewan Whyte is a writer, art and cultural critic. He has written for the *Globe & Mail* and the *Literary Review of Canada*. He is the author of *Desire Lines: Essays on Art, Poetry and Culture*; *Shifting Paradigms: Essays on Art and Culture*; *Entrainment*, a book of poetry; and a translation of the rude ancient Roman poet Catullus. His feature essay "The Cult that Raised Me" on the U.S.-based Community of Jesus/Grenville Christian College cult was a finalist for a National Magazine Award.